facing the wall

Don Potter

Facing the Wall
by Don Potter
Copyright © 2002
2nd Printing, 2006

Distributed by:
Potterhaus Music
PO Box 845
Moravian Falls, NC 28654
www.donpottermusic.com

International Standard Book Number: 1-9786910-0-8

Cover Design by Markus Frehner
Book Layout by Dana Zondory

Unless otherwise indicated, all Scripture quotations are taken from the New American Standard Bible, copyright © 1960, 1962, 1963, 1968, 1971, 1973, 1974, 1977 by The Lockman Foundation. Italics in Scripture are for emphasis only.

No part of this book may be reproduced or transmitted in any form or by any means, electronic or mechanical, including photocopying, recording, or by any information storage and retrieval system, without written permission from the author.

All rights reserved.
Printed in the United States of America.

Contents

5	preface
9	chapter one a little history
13	chapter two prophet/musicians
19	chapter three praise as a strategy
27	chapter four sons of zadok
39	chapter five the musician and the church
55	chapter six anointing
69	chapter seven entertainment
77	chapter eight talent for sale
85	chapter nine the praise life of jesus
95	chapter ten worship leader/transparent person
113	chapter eleven what is an acceptable sacrifice?
117	chapter twelve dipping your hand in the bowl
127	chapter thirteen the practical side of praise
149	appendix seven Hebrew words of praise

preface

In a white two-story farmhouse in upstate New York, there was a gathering of old-timers. They were farmers by day; musicians by night. Carrying their prized instruments under their arms in a wide variety of cases, they came up on the back porch of an old house, single file.

The time was mid-winter about 7 p.m., and it was dark and cold outside, but the wood-burning furnace was stoked up. It got too hot in the house when a lot of people were there so the side door was kept open. Ice-cold air mixed with the humidity of many bodies would collect on the un-insulated windows and freeze in minutes. What a painting. They took positions all over the living room and into the dining room because the upright piano was there. They sat on straight-back chairs brought in from the kitchen. The large opening between the rooms served as a place to stand if you wanted to hear all the players.

Gaius Truman Potter, usually referred to as "G.T.," was the host. He played the fiddle and the washboard. The correct way to play the washboard was to put sewing thimbles on the fingers of the right hand and scratch them along the surface in rhythm with the song. His son, Jerry, had taken violin lessons in high school and learned to read notes so, it was natural for him to lead while others followed these timeless melodies.

Bertha, Jerry's wife, played the piano in the dining room. She had to have her back to everybody because the piano was up against a wall. When she made mistakes, the other musicians would just look at each other and smile and never mention it. It's hard to follow the leader when you have your back to him.

GT was proud of his son, though I never heard him say so. It was easy to see a father's pride when tears would well up after Jerry would play something really great. When he realized a tear was about to fall down his face, he would give a loud laugh and spit in the pail he always kept at his right side.

Right after a good tobacco spit, it was acceptable to wipe your mouth and that gave opportunity to wipe your eyes without notice. In that family, love and approval was a loud laugh and a spit in the pail.

The rest of the musicians in the room couldn't always keep up with Jerry, so they would sometimes just watch him as he sailed off in areas of music they could not comprehend. This would bring another tear to G.T. and soon Jerry would say, "come on you guys, jump in there." The music went on well into the night, and the shouts and laughter would rise higher and higher.

Just when I thought the frost was dancing on the window to the rhythm of the music, my mother would send my brother and me to bed. I was the younger of Jerry's two sons. Even in the upstairs bedrooms of this old house I could still hear every note my father played. I knew his sound no matter how many fiddles were playing, and couldn't close my eyes until he stopped.

My father was a man that everyone loved, but after an affair with a woman who was enamored by a talented musician, he left home.

Mother was mad and hurt at the same time, and decided to bring my brother and me to her mother's until she could get on her feet. Grandma Green's house was only ten miles away from the Potter's, but it felt like a universe. My mother's sister and her husband were also living there with their three kids. The old house was now full with five kids and Grandma Green presiding.

Uncle Bill, my mother's brother-in-law, was a gentle man and almost never laughed very loud, though he was constantly making jokes. He seemed to love kids and cared for my brother and I as well as he cared for his own kids. He had another great quality—he was a musician. Not only could he play the fiddle, but he played the violin as well. He was classically trained and would have a friend over in the evenings and they would play violin duets. They always sat in the kitchen and closed the door to the rest of the house. I would find a way to get into the room and listen. I only knew the sound of hoedowns or square dance music before now, but this music seemed like it could carry your spirit away. Still, I missed my father's sound.

There was a piano in the living room at Grandma Green's house, and I would try to reach the keys to play when I thought no one was around. Though I was only six years old, Uncle Bill felt he could hear something more than a kid banging on a piano. He taught me some chords and would play the fiddle, and I would try to follow him. He kept remarking to Grandma Green about how fast I seemed to learn.

One night, while Grandma was washing dishes in the kitchen, and the rest of the kids were spread out all over the house, I started playing and singing a song I heard in the church Grandma insisted we all attend. "Only Believe" was the title. I figured out the chords and sang the only part of the song I could remember—the last verse and the end. The end was cool because it went up high. As soon as I hit the high note at the end, I could hear my grandmother shouting in the kitchen, "Praise the Lord! Hallelujah!" and her all time favorite phrase, "Mercy me!" She began to worship Jesus right there at the kitchen sink with her soap-covered hands up in the air and tears in her eyes.

After the praising in the kitchen died down, Grandma came into the living room and shouted upstairs. "BILL, GERTRUDE, come down here!" Grandma called my aunt and uncle the same way she called the grandkids. There was a certain cut on the edge of her voice that let you know she meant business. "We've got to pray for this boy right now," Grandma said to my aunt and uncle. She spent a lot of time on her knees in the living room, as did my aunt and uncle, so they automatically took their places. All three began to cry out to God at the same time. "Oh Lord show us how to pray for this boy."

I got on my knees and buried my face in the remaining chair. After awhile they got up, came over to me, laid their hands on me, and began to pray, "Oh Lord, we give this boy over to You and ask that he might never play music unless it is to glorify You."

I had no idea what that prayer would mean in my life. If I had only been a closer friend to wisdom it might not have taken thirty years of prayer to embrace a free gift. I experienced a lot of things while I was in the music business, but I never brought glory to God—only myself.

Finally, after enough prayer from my grandmother, aunt, and uncle, the Lord turned His face toward me and called.

This work is dedicated to the memory of my praising and praying Grandmother. Also to my Aunt Gert and Uncle Bill who took the watch after Grandma died.

chapter one
a little history

PRAISE AND WORSHIP

I was surprised as a new believer to find out what the word "worship" really meant. I thought that singing songs about God was worship. I also thought the louder I sang praise the more God was being worshiped. I went on this way for many years and never asked the question: "Am I really worshiping God or not?" However, I found out that singing is not worshiping God. At the risk of sounding very naive, I'll show you what I found.

Grolier's Encyclopedia defines worship as "a reverent love and devotion for a deity or sacred object, the ceremonies or prayers by which this love is expressed." That was right in alignment with what I thought, but it is not in alignment with what the Bible says. After I got my first Greek/Hebrew concordance, I found something very different about worship.

The Greek word is "proskuneo" meaning to kiss, like a dog at his master's hand, by kneeling to pay homage or expressing respect shown to men and beings of superior rank. The Greeks also use the word "sebomi," which means reverence or respect. There are other Greek words for worship, but these are the most used. There is no mention of love in any of the Greek definitions as it is defined in the encyclopedia.

The Hebrew word "shachah" means to bow down or fall down and is sometimes translated "to fall back." Also, "cegid" which means to prostrate oneself. Again, there is no mention of a ceremony by which love is expressed.

There is no doubt it is important to worship God; in fact we are commanded to worship the Lord (see Matthew 4:10, Deuteronomy 6:13). However, to truly worship God one must be ready to bow low and serve. We are also commanded to love the Lord our God with all our heart, soul and mind (see Matthew 22:36-37). Is singing songs about the Lord on Sunday bringing Him worship and love? I won't try to answer that for you, but I realized—I needed a change.

SATAN WANTED TO BE WORSHIPED

> **Again, the devil took Him to a very high mountain, and showed Him all the kingdoms of the world, and their glory;**
>
> **and he said to Him, "All these things will I give You, if You fall down and worship me."**
>
> **Then Jesus said to him, "Begone, Satan! For it is written, 'You shall worship the Lord your God, and serve Him only'" (Matthew 4:8-10).**

When the devil tries to get Jesus to bow before him, the Greek translates "worship" with two words. Proskuneo, which means to kiss the hand, and enopion, which means to look at the face or respond to the presence of someone. Satan wanted Jesus to recognize his presence as someone worthy of service with the goal of getting others to seek his face instead of the face of God. The battle we are still in is the enemy's efforts to get us to serve or worship him and not the Lord. The devil is not asking anyone to love him, only to work for him.

As I said earlier, I thought I was worshiping and serving the Lord when I sang some songs to Him in church. Meanwhile I serve and work for men and even pay homage to them to stimulate good relations. What would happen if you went to work one day and sang to your boss instead of doing what he pays you for? This all means that it is time to understand God must be worshiped, which means served and reverenced; loved, which means relationship, closeness, and friendship; and praised, which I will try to define later.

God is not being completely worshiped if I say, "I love You," and do not obey His Word (see Luke 6:46-49). There is action involved with worship, and serving is the heart of that action.

Praise and worship are definitely different from each other, and I want to bring a little more clarity to this word so I can better explain praise.

PRAISE

Praise is a completely different word, and making a sacrifice or offering of praise has a deep meaning to God as well as the believer.

Sacrifice and offering mean the same. When Christians come together to praise the Lord, they are making an offering of praise to God. When looking at the meaning of sacrifice or offering, we see another connotation hidden in these words.

SACRIFICE OR OFFERING

"Qorban" is the Hebrew word for offering. It means oblation or sacrifice, and it has a root word that is "garab." This means to offer as to come or draw near, bring nigh, approach, or enter into. To make an offering or a sacrifice of praise to God means you desire to draw near to Him. That's why He takes these offerings so seriously.

If you desire to have a relationship with someone, you will have to make some sacrifices for that relationship to survive. Your sacrifices are seen as a desire to draw near. Sunday morning church is the time that is traditionally set aside for this purpose. Though your heart is full of joy when you see someone once a week, there can be no deep relationship until there has been a sacrifice to show the depths of your desire to know them. If you haven't made it through at least one hard time with someone, chances are that relationship is only on the surface. This is what can happen to our relationship with God if we are only looking for Him on Sunday. I want to encourage believers to bring your sacrifice of praise with the hope of drawing near to God and developing a closer relationship with Him in the bargain.

It is becoming clearer to me as time goes on that God invested something in His people Israel concerning praise that I'm only just learning about. For example, English translations of the Bible use the word praise, whereas the Hebrew uses many different words to express praise. The Jews of the Bible have seldom been afraid to show their feelings or emotions about God in their praise of Him. They have been known to dance with all their might before Him, fall on the ground and cover themselves with dirt as a show of repentance, shout at the top of their lungs a victory shout, and openly mourn for the sins of another—many passions that some are too afraid to feel.

Our example of praise is given to us in the Old Testament, and I don't believe God has changed His mind on how He wants to be praised.

chapter two
prophet/musicians

Musicians have been referred to as many different things over the years—prophet has not been one of them. This is not to say that all musicians are called to be prophets, but it is possible for a musician to prophesy in song.

I found in I Samuel 10, that the prophet Samuel had followers who were training under him. These men were musicians who walked in the office of prophet as well as minstrel. *Strong's Greek/Hebrew Dictionary* defines prophet like this.

PROPHET= NABI (Hebrew) *speaker of oracles, one who was actuated by a divine Spirit. In the time of Samuel, there were men who followed him, praising God in song and attempting to call the people back to God.*

When I read this definition, I realized the reason music has such an attracting power about it. Music has the power to call people. It has the strength to turn heads and change hearts. It can also turn people back to God, and I believe that is still its purpose.

Once I was leading praise at a Friday night service where there were a lot of young people. Everyone was having a great time jumping up and down and singing, except for one girl. She wasn't just another kid having a bad day, but someone who looked very rough and seriously depressed.

I try not to look at people when I lead as it is often too distracting, but I couldn't get my eyes off this discouraged girl.

Without warning, I began to sing prophetically and I realized God wanted to speak to this brokenhearted girl. Some of the people started to look at me like I was losing it, because nothing seemed to make sense. We were singing a song of joy, and in the middle of it, I started singing all these depressing statements.

After awhile, the dancing let up and more were wondering what was happening. Finally the girl began to break and started to weep. She all but collapsed when someone in the crowd that noticed the interaction came to her and led her to Jesus. This was a clear example of how music and the prophetic can be used to call the people back to God.

There are biblical examples of prophetic music having an affect on people. In I Samuel 10, Samuel gave Saul instructions to go and meet his small band of prophet/musicians and experience what God has given them.

> **"After that you will go to Gibeah of God, where there is a Philistine outpost. As you approach the town, you will meet a procession of prophets coming down from the high place with lyres, tambourines, flutes and harps being played before them, and they will be prophesying.**
>
> **The Spirit of the LORD will come upon you in power, and you will prophesy with them; and you will be changed into a different person"** (I Samuel 10:5-6 NIV).

This shows that there is power in the prophetic musician for the changing of men's hearts. However, another thing must happen before a man's life goes through real change.

> **And it was so, that when he (Saul) had turned his back to go from Samuel, God gave him another heart: and all those signs came to pass that day** (I Samuel 10:9 KJV).

Now in verse 10 it says the Spirit of the Lord came on Saul when he saw the company of prophet/musicians. If God had not changed his heart, Saul would not have been able to receive from the Holy Spirit.

It's important to keep the role of music in these Scriptures in the right perspective. The music was the vehicle used to bring Saul into a place in the Spirit he had never been before. But if God had not changed his heart first, then the Holy Spirit would not have been realized in the fullest way. Without the heart change, the music would have just provided a nice background.

Music or even praise will just be background sound if God does not change the heart. With that change in place, then music can become a vehicle for prophecy, praise, healing, protection, and many more things in the Lord.

In spite of this life-changing event, Saul later embraced jealousy and fear of displacement to the point of ordering David to be taken. Now the very same prophet/musicians would be used by God to be a protection for His anointed.

> **And Saul sent messengers to take David: and when they saw the company of the prophets prophesying, and Samuel standing as appointed over them, the Spirit of God was upon the messengers of Saul, and they also prophesied.**
>
> **And when it was told Saul, he sent other messengers, and they prophesied likewise. And Saul sent messengers again the third time, and they prophesied also (I Samuel 19:20-21 KJV).**

Saul went himself to this place to take David and he also prophesied. Scripture says Saul stripped himself, fell on the ground and spoke the word of God all night (see I Samuel 19:24). The Spirit of the Lord came on Saul like it did on the other men sent to take David. There was no fighting or words exchanged. Once again, Saul's experience with the prophet/musicians was life-changing.

Whoever God chooses or anoints to do His will have come under some kind of attack. It started with Cain and Abel, and continued through to Jesus, and is still happening today. Saul was simply being controlled by this spirit. The weapon to use when jealousy, envy, and strife are starting to come against you is prophetic praise as this is a spiritual war. Remember that the testimony of Jesus is the spirit of prophecy (see Revelation 19:10). Moving in the prophetic should be evidence of Jesus.

PROPHETIC PRAISE CAN CHANGE THE HEART

The new song that is spoken of in Psalms is a divinely inspired word from God set to music. (TeHILLAH: refer to the seven Hebrew words.) David tells of the power this has.

> **He put a new song in my mouth, a hymn of praise to our God. Many will see and fear and put their trust in the LORD (Psalm 40:3 NIV).**

The word **"fear"** used by David has more meaning than just being afraid. It is described as a very positive feeling of awe or reverence for God and can be expressed in worship. It also means to tremble. That kind of reverence causes people's hearts to change.

When someone is worshiping in Spirit and in Truth, the new song will become a prophetic sound, and those hearing it can be touched and brought to a trembling reverence for God, then to a place of trusting in the Lord. I believe David gained this knowledge from his experiences with Samuel and the prophet/musician band.

I Corinthians 14:24-25 says something similar as Paul instructs the Corinthian church.

> **But if an unbeliever or someone who does not understand comes in while everybody is prophesying, he will be convinced by all that he is a sinner and will be judged by all,**
>
> **and the secrets of his heart will be laid bare. So he will fall down and worship God, exclaiming, "God is really among you!" (I Corinthians 14:24-25 NIV).**

I experienced a brief moment of this during that Friday night meeting I mentioned earlier. The song the Lord had divinely inspired touched the young girl and she gave her life to Jesus. Remember the Scripture **"while everybody is prophesying?"** The only way I know that everyone can prophesy at the same time is during praise when all start singing in the Spirit. Let me explain.

Paul's instructions in I Corinthians 14:22 says that prophecy is for those who believe—not for the unbeliever. Then in verse 24 he says if everyone is prophesying and an unbeliever comes in he will be convicted of his sin and say God is really among you.

The way these can both be true is if one of them is done in a corporate way, i.e. singing in the Spirit. After all, singing in the Spirit is singing by divine inspiration and that is the definition of prophecy. At the end of *Strong's Dictionary* definition of prophecy it says, "a poet, because poets were believed to have sung by divine inspiration." This is how the unbeliever will be touched when he or she comes into the house of the Lord. It seems to me that God is still calling prophetic musicians.

For years believers have been looking for an additional way to evangelize. This approach has a lot of controversy surrounding it and has even been abandoned by much of the Christian church. We are given the tools we need to do the will of God. If we decide, through judging others, that some of these tools shouldn't be used, then we limit the work of salvation and the number of souls that could be changed by the experience.

chapter three
praise as a strategy

When Saul was touched by the Spirit as the prophet/musicians ministered to him, a great mystery was unveiled. When David was being pursued by Saul and found protection in the midst of prophetic praise, a strategy was realized. This strategy is not only for protection, but for spiritual warfare as well.

These Scriptures will reveal how the Lord gave Judah a divine strategy to overcome their enemies.

> **After this, the Moabites and Ammonites with some of the Meunites came to make war on Jehoshaphat.**
>
> **Some men came and told Jehoshaphat, "A vast army is coming against you from Edom, from the other side of the Sea. It is already in Hazazon Tamar" (that is, En Gedi) (II Chronicles 20:1-2, NIV).**
>
> **Then Jehoshaphat stood up in the assembly of Judah and Jerusalem at the temple of the LORD in the front of the new courtyard**
>
> **and said: "O LORD, God of our fathers, are you not the God who is in heaven? You rule over all the kingdoms of the nations. Power and might are in your hand, and no one can withstand you" (II Chronicles 20:5-6 NIV).**

Then Jehoshaphat proclaimed a fast for all of Judah and they sought the Lord earnestly.

> **Then the Spirit of the LORD came upon Jahaziel son of Zechariah, the son of Benaiah, the son of Jeiel, the son of Mattaniah, a Levite and descendant of Asaph, as he stood in the assembly (II Chronicles 20:14 NIV).**

Being a descendent of Asaph means this man was a singer and a review of his lineage proves he was known among the leaders. He wasn't a stranger in the crowd offering an encouraging word in this time of struggle. This is important.

> **He said: "Listen, King Jehoshaphat and all who live in Judah and Jerusalem! This is what the LORD says to you: 'Do not be afraid or discouraged because of this vast army. For the battle is not yours, but God's.**
>
> **Tomorrow march down against them. They will be climbing up by the Pass of Ziz, and you will find them at the end of the gorge in the Desert of Jeruel.**
>
> **You will not have to fight this battle. Take up your positions; stand firm and see the deliverance the LORD will give you, O Judah and Jerusalem. Do not be afraid; do not be discouraged. Go out to face them tomorrow, and the LORD will be with you'" (II Chronicles 20:15-17 NIV).**

Would a nation listen to a singer, possibly singing this word, when so much was at stake? He would probably not be heard, unless he was known and trusted, and the power of the Lord was on the word. All this must have been in place because the king believed him.

> **Early in the morning they left for the Desert of Tekoa. As they set out, Jehoshaphat stood and said, "Listen to me, Judah and people of Jerusalem! Have faith in the LORD your God and you will be upheld; have faith in his prophets and you will be successful" (II Chronicles 20:20 NIV).**

This Scripture clearly states that having faith in God upholds us, but having faith in His prophets brings us success. Being upheld by God means being assured, believed, and supported—all the things we cannot do for ourselves. Success means to push forward, break out, or to go over. Trusting God is a two-part deal. First, be assured by believing in God and second, push forward by believing in what God is doing. God meets us in our faith, but we must walk out our lives believing He is our deliverer, yet He uses man in His plans.

It is more difficult for me to trust when God uses men in my life. However, I have learned it is important to really know that person and trust their walk with the Lord. That is done by examining the fruit of their lives. Jahaziel was the fruit of generations of trusted prophets.

> **And when he had consulted with the people, he appointed those who sang to the Lord and those who praised** (Yadah) **Him in holy attire, as they went out before the army and said, "Give thanks to the Lord, for His lovingkindness is everlasting" (II Chronicles 20:21).**

God did not give Jehoshaphat the strategy of sending the singers out in front of the army. He determined that to happen after he consulted with the people. Was this a divine revelation, or did he think grateful praise couldn't hurt a thing right now? I think Jehoshaphat felt such an anointing on this word given by a praising Levite that he decided praise was the strategy.

WARNING ABOUT SPIRITUAL WARFARE

Years ago, I was going to an early morning intercession meeting. I drove by a palm reading place and decided to curse it and quickly cast that demon out of the city. I was feeling powerful as I was gearing up for the intercession time. I spent the next five years suffering from my fingertips splitting open and bleeding uncontrollably. Since I made a living as a studio guitar player at that time, this could have very seriously hurt my career.

As it was, I had to hide my hands from the producers I worked for. If they even so much as thought I couldn't perform at top level at all times, I would be fired. It took five years of praying and trying every remedy the doctors could think of before the Lord took this away. Just as suddenly as it came on me, it left. That was a stern warning not to take spiritual warfare too lightly. Godly wisdom must be applied at all times. Under the direction of the Holy Spirit, the Father will show us where and when to stand against His enemies.

Praise doesn't fight any battles; however, it will bless the Mighty Warrior. In the midst of that praise, verse 22 shows us what the Lord does to His enemies.

> **As they began to sing and praise,** (TeHILLAH) **the LORD set ambushes against the men of Ammon and Moab and Mount Seir who were invading Judah, and they were defeated.**
>
> **The men of Ammon and Moab rose up against the men from Mount Seir to destroy and annihilate them. After they finished slaughtering the men from Seir, they helped to destroy one another.**
>
> **When the men of Judah came to the place that overlooks the desert and looked toward the vast army, they saw only dead bodies lying on the ground; no one had escaped (II Chronicles 20:22-24 NIV).**

THE MEANING OF THESE WORDS

The Lord never wastes words in the Scriptures. As you look at the meanings of some of these words it will give better insight into what Judah was facing, and also what we have faced and will be facing in the future.

Most of us know that JUDAH means praise, or the praising people of God, which says this attack was against praise. In verse 19, praise is the Hebrew word HALAL (refer to "Seven Hebrew Words of Praise"). After some of the Levites heard the word of the Lord concerning deliverance from their enemy, they began to praise God in HALAL praise. This word is defined as boasting in the Lord, celebrating, being clamorously foolish, and being radiant. These men, while facing death, were bragging on their Father's power.

In verse 21, Jehoshaphat appointed men to sing to the Lord and praise. This time the word praise is YADAH (refer to "Seven

Hebrew Words of Praise"). It means being thankful for the blessings in your life. This is also the word that was used by David for confessing the Holiness of God, as well as confessing his sins. This was done publicly in some cases. With the situation that the men of Judah and Jehoshaphat were facing, I'll bet the confessing of their sins was right at the top of the praise list. This will need to be at the top of our praise list, too, if we are going to walk out the divine strategies God has planned for us.

The root word of YADAH is the word YADA. This goes a lot deeper into the heart of the one who praises. This is the word used for intimate knowing. In the struggle to not be overcome by our enemies, there will be no better weapon offered to us than an intimate knowing of God. That can only come by allowing us to be known by God—opening our hearts before Him as a regular practice.

In verse 22, the singers began to praise in TeHILLAH praise (refer to "Seven Hebrew Words of Praise"). This was done right on the battlefield. They sang their hymns and laudations to the Lord. This is the praise the Lord inhabits (see Psalm 22:3).

WHO IS THE ENEMY?

If we look at the word Judah as praise or "the praising people of God", we see that the same enemy that came against God's praising people back then are the same spirits that come against us now. The nations that were coming against Judah were the Ammonites, Moabites, and the people of Mt. Seir, (which consisted of the Horites, Esauites, or Edomites).

Moab was the son born to Lot and his eldest daughter. Ammon was the descendent of Ben-Ammi, the younger son born to Lot and his younger daughter (see Genesis 19:31-38). Lot's daughters determined that they would not have children like the women of the world because of their quick departure from Sodom and Gomorrah. So they both decided to take matters into their own hands.

So both of Lot's daughters became pregnant by their father.

> The older daughter had a son, and she named him Moab; he is the father of the Moabites of today.
>
> The younger daughter also had a son, and she named him Ben-ammi; he is the father of the Ammonites of today. (Genesis 19:36-38 NIV).

Moab was also known as "the posterity of the preceding." I won't even try to define that, but-it is safe to say these people were not friends of Judah. In fact, they were rejected by Israel, were conquered by David, rebelled after Ahab's death, and defeated again when their king offered his son as a sacrifice.

Mt. Seir had a few nations within her borders. The Horites were the original inhabitants of Mt. Seir.

> Horites used to live in Seir, but the descendants of Esau drove them out. They destroyed the Horites from before them and settled in their place, just as Israel did in the land the LORD gave them as their possession (Deuteronomy 2:12 NIV).

The Horites would make their homes in the rocks by excavating many holes in the sandstone cliffs and mountains of Edom. The rock that is best known for their many dwellings is called "Petra." You could say that the Horites were known for their erosion or making holes in the rock.

It seems as though the spiritual enemies we face are trying to erode a hole in the Rock of our salvation. Jesus said it was on this Rock that He would build His church (see Matthew 16:18). It's the praise and gratefulness of the church that is under an attack of erosion.

Then the descendants of Esau came and took over the eroded places in the rock and made them their homes. Remember, Esau hated his brother (see Genesis 27:41). If we survive the erosion of our faith, we must be aware that he who hates his brother will come and take over that place, and you will be faced with a worse enemy—resentment and bitterroot judgments.

IS THIS HAPPENING TO US?

Are the praising people of God suffering the threat of attack from the spirits of perversion, incest, selfishness, and the erosion of the Rock of our salvation? I believe the answer is yes. The devil is attacking the praising people of God from every angle he can.

Repenting was a strong part of the warfare for Judah. The first part of the battle plan was to pray, (on their faces). The second part was to praise God in (HALAL) praise when He revealed His divine strategy. The third part was to confess their sins (YADAH). The fourth part was taking their positions and standing strong, which was gratefully praising God (TeHILLAH) for the beauty of His Holiness. This is the same order of events that took place when David brought the Ark up into the temple.

You may never feel that praise should be used as a tool for warfare. I didn't either, until the enemies of God came after me with such a vengeance that I didn't know where to turn. Only when I lifted my voice in prayer, and then went wild praising the Lord with gratefulness, did I experience any peace. Once in awhile I forget this and have to be reminded again.

chapter four
sons of zadok

The Zadok priesthood may never completely return as it once was, but there will always be those who minister before the Lord. What I will point out in this chapter is not intended to discourage a praise leader, but to challenge. The job of ministering before the Lord is not a laborious one of impossible rules to remember, but one of playing and singing your best, still reaching past yourself in the creative energy that He alone can provide. No matter what your musical ability, it must be your best, still reaching.

The sons of Zadok were Levites that proved themselves to be faithful to the Lord. As a result of their faithfulness, they were allowed to come near to the presence of God and minister to Him. When I first read about them in Scripture, I didn't think it would have anything to do with today's praise leaders. But it does.

First let me give you some history on their father. Zadok (meaning "righteous") was a Levite high priest, faithful to King David when Adonijah rebelled. He stayed true to David during Adonijah's usurpation. He was also known for carrying the Ark of the Covenant with Abiathar, following King David in his flight from his son Absalom (see II Samuel 15:24).

While David was hidden, he sent Zadok back to Jerusalem to worship in the tabernacle, all the time spying on Absalom. Zadok's sons brought the information back to David. King David was anointed and had the Holy Spirit on him. Zadok and his sons were faithful to the anointing and the Holy Spirit, no matter who was on the throne. That was the beginning of the Zadok reputation of faithfulness.

I know it is popular today to call the musicians in the church Levites. Nevertheless, I believe it would be beneficial for all those that consider themselves Levites to study the requirements that they faced. I want to share some of the things I found while studying this tribe.

UNFAITHFUL LEVITES

> **"'The Levites who went far from me when Israel went astray and who wandered from me after their idols must bear the consequences of their sin.**
>
> **They may serve in my sanctuary, having charge of the gates of the temple and serving in it; they may slaughter the burnt offerings and sacrifices for the people and stand before the people and serve them.**
>
> **But because they served them in the presence of their idols and made the house of Israel fall into sin, therefore I have sworn with uplifted hand that they must bear the consequences of their sin, declares the Sovereign LORD'" (Ezekiel 44:10-12 NIV).**

This Scripture clearly states that serving God's people in the presence of an idol caused a whole nation to fall into sin. The word "idol" means the image of something. That doesn't only mean a wooden statue on the stage. If performance or entertainment is an idol to the musicians on stage, it will cause the people to fall into sin. The sin is giving attention to a false god. It truly is the job of the praise leader to encourage the people to worship God alone, and anything else is idol worship.

There is a consequence for those that lead in front of an idol, even the idol of ambition. Verse 13 makes it very clear.

> **They are not to come near to serve me as priests or come near any of my holy things or my most**

> **holy offerings; they must bear the shame of their detestable practices.**
>
> **Yet I will put them in charge of the duties of the temple and all the work that is to be done in it (Ezekiel 44:13-14 NIV).**

In these two verses, it says a Levite can work in the church and do many things to serve the people and still not be allowed to come close to the Lord. If any of the idols I mentioned above are present in the musicians of today, then the One who is needed most in ministry will distance Himself from those ministering. In other words, don't expect the Lord to come mightily while you minister if you have selfish ambition.

IDOLS

There were many times in Judah's history that kings let idol worship get in the way, but I believe the Lord is referring to a particular incident. Let me explain.

In II Kings 22 and 23, the eight-year-old boy Josiah was made king of Judah. When he was eighteen years old, the book of the covenant was found in the temple. He heard the reading of the Law for the first time. When he heard his own name mentioned in the reading of the Law, his reaction was very strong.

> **And it came to pass, when the king had heard the words of the book of the law, that he rent his clothes (II Kings 22:11 KJV).**

In his excitement, he commanded one of the priests to inquire of the Lord.

> **Go ye, inquire of the LORD for me, and for the people, and for all Judah, concerning the words of this book that is found: for great is the wrath of the LORD that is kindled against us, because our fathers have not hearkened unto the words of this book, to do according unto all that which is written concerning us (II Kings 22:13 KJV).**

After hearing from God and how angry the unfaithfulness had made Him, Josiah began tearing down the high places.

Even the holy temple had idols in it, but there is no record of the Levite priests standing in opposition. They were the teachers of the Law and still did not object to the worship of idols right in the temple. Why did they let this happen?

PRAISE LEADERS TODAY

It is my belief the praise leaders of today need to know the Word well enough and have a close relationship with God and to recognize an ambitious spirit, an idol, or anything that tries to exalt itself above the knowledge of God. That leader must deal with those spirits as soon as they are identified.

I was made head of the praise department of a church one time and I noticed some spiritual things that were not good in the musicians that had been there a long time. Ambition, lust, and elitism were beginning to manifest. I decided not to say anything, hoping it would just go away. I also struggled with my own versions of these same spirits and didn't feel confident enough to bring correction to someone else when I couldn't be sure it wasn't just my own stuff.

As time went on, this became worse and it began to affect the church. By the time I started to deal with this, it was too late. I was being accused of the very things I saw on others. This led to division and almost completely destroyed the friendships that were developing. I stepped down from the position knowing I was the only one guilty.

After a year of seeking the Lord on where I went wrong He simply said, "you should have dealt with these things as soon as they were revealed to you." He went on to say that I was the leader and it was my responsibility to deal with what the Lord revealed to me in those under me. If I suffered the same problems, He would be faithful to show them to me through those who were over me.

God is governmental, and He won't disrupt that bureaucracy even if the leadership is in error. However, He will deal with errant leadership more harshly if there is no repentance. If you are the praise leader, you must deal with the things the Lord reveals to you, when He reveals them.

Today's Idols

For what happened to the Levites in Judah to happen today may seem impossible, but if you look at the reasons that led up to their unfaithfulness, you'll find that some of the same things can happen today. The idol worship that the Levites fell prey to did not happen all at once. It took years of one little compromise after another to arrive at this.

Israel began going astray when it was politically wise to show honor to the gods of other nations they allied with. They did this when help was needed to conquer an attacking force. It was the political spirit and self-reliance that began to erode Israel's leaders. Saul was the first king of Israel and the first to rely on his own sense of right and wrong. He trusted his own interpretation of the commands of God.

Interesting note: God never intended for Israel to have a "king." When He spoke to Samuel and told him to anoint Saul He said, "Anoint him commander or leader of My people" (see I Samuel 9:16, I Samuel 10:1). Commander, prince, or captain means someone with power, but who is under authority. The elders of Israel demanded a king and even after a warning from God through Samuel (see I Samuel 8:9), they still wanted a king instead of a commander.

The word "king" means royalty. That's a person with no authority over him. That is a position that should be reserved for God alone. Though this seems like a subtle difference, it is the reason Saul and many other kings after him fell from grace. Without some kind of accountability, even a king will fall into error.

Kings Who Did Evil

I could list king after king that brought some kind of perversion to the statutes and commands of God, and most of those reasons will ultimately be dealing with political positioning. Starting with Saul, with the exclusion of David, many of the kings of Israel and Judah fought to hold on to the power of the throne. They were not willing to rely on or wait on God for strength. Slowly, year after year, they drifted away from the statutes and commands of the Lord.

The Levite priests were the teachers of the Law and of the commands of God. They were also the gatekeepers, which means they were the protection for the holy things inside of the temple. Why didn't they object to these compromises of the truth and the onslaught of idols being put in the temple? What power caused them to embrace these changes? I believe it was a political spirit. Everyone would benefit from these small concessions.

Today the enemies we face are principalities and powers in high places. We must still rely on God alone for power, but it is often difficult waiting for His timing.

POLITICAL SPIRIT

Let me try to explain what I believe the political spirit is. The political spirit is self-promotion, self-reliance, and self-preservation. I've heard it called aligning yourself with as many powerful people as possible for the potential favor that can be gained from the association. The same thing can happen in ministry, only it is a bit more difficult to recognize.

Some will try to associate themselves with an anointing someone else has. First, because of the benefits of the association and second, they believe they need that anointing to carry out their own desire to minister.

It is my "opinion" that trying to associate oneself with the anointing or the gifting on another for the purpose of gaining credibility through the association is the root of the political spirit.

If you study the kings of Israel and Judah from Solomon to Josiah, you will see a continuous reduction of the holiness that was once Israel. When Josiah started honoring Passover again, it was realized that there hadn't been a Passover celebrated since the days of the judges of Israel (see II Kings 23:22). That means all the kings of Israel didn't deem it important to obey that command from God (see Exodus 12:17). Even when certain kings would try to do what was right in the sight of the Lord, there were still some false idols left in place.

ALLOWED TO COME CLOSE

> "'But the priests, who are Levites and descendants of Zadok and who faithfully carried out the duties of my sanctuary when the Israelites went astray from me, are to come near to minister before me; they are to stand before me to offer sacrifices of fat and blood, declares the Sovereign LORD.
>
> They alone are to enter my sanctuary; they alone are to come near my table to minister before me and perform my service'" (Ezekiel 44:15-16 NIV).

I've always thought that I had to do something that would bring the presence of the Lord. Now I see that He is always there and it is me that needs to draw close to Him. Only faithfulness will accomplish that.

> And without faith it is impossible to please him. For whoever would draw near to God must believe that he exists and that he rewards those who seek him (Hebrews 11:6 RSV).

Remember, drawing near means sacrifice or offering. Our sacrifice of praise is our hope of drawing near to God (see Chapter 1, the definition of praise).

ASSUMING A HIGH POSITION

> "If you are invited to a wedding feast, don't always head for the best seat. What if someone more respected than you has also been invited?
>
> The host will say, 'Let this person sit here instead.' Then you will be embarrassed and will have to take whatever seat is left at the foot of the table!
>
> "Do this instead — sit at the foot of the table. Then when your host sees you, he will come and say, 'Friend, we have a better place than this for you!' Then you will be honored in front of all the other guests.

For the proud will be humbled, but the humble will be honored" (Luke 14:8-11 NLT).

"**Feast**" in Luke 14:8 means "entertainment." Jesus is giving us the protocol for feasts and banquets. Both words can be found under the one word "entertainment" in the *Greek Lexicon*.

Once when I was in California at a music awards show, the backstage area was buzzing with one star after another. I was there performing with an act that was hoping for an award. With that many famous people in one room it is pointless for anyone to expect preferential treatment. All of a sudden, bodyguards and bouncers came into the backstage area and began pushing all these well-known artists out of the way so the star they worked for wouldn't be bothered by presumed fans. As you can imagine, after that the talk among the rest of the music community was not good, and the artist in question soon became unknown to the public.

This was one of the most presumptuous things this artist could have done. Pride does precede a fall, even in the world.

When entertainers or praise bands come together, they must start by taking a lowly seat first. Then, if the head of that meeting chooses to lift you up, it will be done with true honor and not from self-promotion. (I will write more on entertainment in the chapter called "Entertainment.")

QUESTION

What would a Zadok priesthood look like today? Before I try to answer that let me show you what the Lord has to say.

For this is what the LORD says: 'David will never fail to have a man to sit on the throne of the house of Israel,

nor will the priests, who are Levites, ever fail to have a man to stand before me continually to offer burnt offerings, to burn grain offerings and to present sacrifices'" (Jeremiah 33:17-18 NIV).

"Burnt offerings" mean ascending or a stairway—something that ascends on the smoke rising from the offering. Grain offerings are like gifts or tributes, a present. Though burnt offerings or blood offerings are no longer required, what they represented still is. It continues to be important to ascend to the Lord and to bring gifts and tribute to Him. There is no escaping the reality, offering a sacrifice of praise to God still has some requirements.

Today, the sacrifice is the sacrifice of praise. The faithful Levites are to prepare that sacrifice skillfully and deliberately to make it acceptable to God. He will come as a refiner's fire to purify those that minister before Him so that the sacrifice they offer will be righteous before Him.

> **"And He will sit as a smelter and purifier of silver, and He will purify the sons of Levi and refine them like gold and silver, so that they may present to the LORD offerings in righteousness.**
>
> **"Then the offering of Judah and Jerusalem will be pleasing to the LORD, as in the days of old and as in former years" (Malachi 3:3-4).**

THE BLOOD OF JESUS

All these Scriptures make it sound like no one could fulfill the requirements set forth, and for the most part that is true.

The shedding of the blood of Jesus rent the curtain that kept everyone out of the Holy of Holies. Now we have access, but only through the blood and the cross. It is a repentant heart and an open confession of His Lordship that qualifies us to enter His gates with thanksgiving and His courts with praise. Once we have entered that place, we are faced with what kind of sacrifice we bring.

I don't mean how good is the music, though that is important, but what condition is the heart of the praise leader and the group? Is this a whole-hearted act of praise and sacrifice to the Lord?

The blood of Jesus did not lower God's requirements for a pure sacrifice. In fact, it raised the standard higher than ever before. One drop of Messiah's blood accomplished more than all of the previous sacrifices. With such an awesome gift we must never take lightly the position of leader of the sacrifice of praise.

REQUIRED TO TEACH

> **And they** (faithful Levites) **shall teach my people the difference between the holy and profane, and cause them to discern between the unclean and the clean (Ezekiel 44:23 KJV).**

This Scripture says that the faithful Levites were to teach. Unfaithfulness will cloud one's ability to distinguish the difference between holy and profane. The Levites in Ezekiel's time taught the Law. Today we teach by our actions and what we have gained from our relationship with Jesus. If the praise leaders of today are to lead God's people into a place of sacrifice, then they will need a strong grasp on the Word (see II Timothy 2:15).

They are still required to teach the difference between the holy and the profane. Something that is holy is set apart or sanctified. Something that is profane is that which has a common use or is unholy. Our praise must never become common or unholy, but set aside and sanctified for the Lord.

Joseph Garlington says, "Somehow it doesn't seem accurate to use the same word to describe our God as we do our favorite high fat food." That is discerning the difference between the holy and the profane.

PARABLE OF THE TALENTS

Read Matthew 25:14-30. These are the Scriptures that tell the story of the servants that were given talents according to their abilities. The Lord began to impress on me to look at these Scriptures with the idea of the talents not only meaning money, but talent itself.

The first two men invested and doubled their talents, and gained access to the rewards of a king. The last man buried his talent and the Master in anger said; **"Well, you should at least have put my money into the bank so I could have some interest" (Matthew 25:27 NLT).** The word **"least"** means the least one can do with their talent is to draw interest on it. Trying to make money or gain interest from your talent is not the worst thing you can do with it—it's the least you can do with it. If you invest in your talent, then it will grow. The growth was what pleased the returning Master, not the amount.

The principle that I'm trying to explain here is a simple one. Someone who ministers to God's people must first set all of his or her talents at the feet of Jesus and then allow themselves to be used in a way that pleases God. Then it is wise stewarding to invest in your talent. Practically speaking, that means improving. Because the Holy Spirit used you in a mighty way once doesn't mean you should be satisfied with what you are offering God. God is satisfied with your best, and can only be pleased when it is offered in faith. That best should be growing every day. This is how to give the Spirit a larger vocabulary when He uses you. God is still creating.

chapter five
the musician and the church

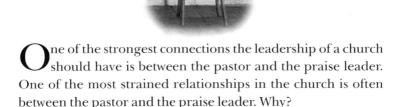

One of the strongest connections the leadership of a church should have is between the pastor and the praise leader. One of the most strained relationships in the church is often between the pastor and the praise leader. Why?

The answer is so complicated, that I won't even try. What I can do is give some examples of my own experiences and hope they are relatable.

Being a professional musician for thirty-six years has kept me from experiencing the idiosyncrasies of the musician in the church. However, when I did start playing in church with other musicians and leading praise, I only saw things from the perspective of the musician.

Now being in ministry, my perspective is broadening. I'm slowly seeing why there is so much tension between the leadership of the church and the musician. It is basically a lack of trust. Some pastors feel musicians cannot be completely trusted. The idea of giving a musician freedom to sing what he or she feels and play what seems right to them is quite a stretch. On the other hand, the musicians want to be submissive to their pastor, but not to the concepts of someone they don't musically respect. Neither side is willing to trust that the other is consistently hearing from God, so this strain continues on and the only victor is the devil.

I have experienced a misuse of authority on some occasions when a leader doesn't personally like a music style and is unable to admit it. He then goes to the musicians and says this music is not of God. We are all guilty of holding our own opinions in higher esteem than we should. Musicians will sometimes fight for what they think is right and it becomes a battle of opinions.

Again the only victor is the devil.

MUSICIANS WHO USE THE CHURCH

When I speak of a musician in the church, I mean someone God has clearly placed an anointing on to play the instrument in an attitude of praise. I'm not referring to those who appointed themselves to the role of leadership.

Knowing when that musician has come fully into that anointing is not easily discerned. This is because the musician God has anointed is usually also talented. His talent can make it seem as though he is already there. Someone's talent often puts him or her in a place that his or her character cannot sustain. (I'll talk about the anointed musician in later chapters.)

When musicians or even athletes start becoming well-known, he or she gains a credibility that they didn't really earn. Their talent, in that one area, has given them a platform for which many look to for guidance. The talented musician in the church will give the same impression.

Just being able to play an instrument does not qualify anyone to lead praise, or even be part of a worship team. A closer look at the heart is what is required.

Some musicians, frustrated with how their careers are going, will use the church for their own selfish gain. The talented ones will sometimes live in the fantasy of getting famous, and try to walk out that fantasy in front of a congregation that is desirous to worship. Some of the not-so-talented players feel they could not make it in the world, so they use the church to fulfill their desire for audience acceptance. This sounds a little harsh I know, and the ones I'm talking about are really in the minority, but that small group is making it harder and harder for the leadership of the church to trust the musician.

SUGGESTIONS

Let me offer some suggestions to the leadership in charge of music, based solely on my own impressions and experiences. These are things to look for in the people you are considering for the job of praise leader, singer, or musician in the band.

1. Move slowly with anyone who is too anxious to be on the worship team. See if they are willing to serve the church by interceding for the music people for a period of time.

2. Don't be so sure a bigger band is better.

3. Find out if the person you are considering has a stable family life. Being involved with the praise band will put a strain on their families.

4. Watch carefully the ones who are too willing to sacrifice everything to be there on Sunday. Some have a greater need to perform than to serve God.

5. If you have a trusted worship leader, try to get him or her to nurture and groom someone else for that job. That keeps the church from being overly dependent on one person, and gives the leader time to seek God for direction.

6. Be sure not to bring a really talented musician into the worship band too soon after he or she arrives in the church. Though you may need their talent desperately, they may be just looking for some peace from the demands that others have put on their talent. Wait for the Lord to release them in praise.

7. It is okay to ask someone to audition. Each musician you add to a band must contribute spiritually and musically to it, not burden it. (Notice I said spiritually AND musically. If you leave one of those out of the requirement, there will be consequences.)

Worshiping Talent

I've been using the words "talent" and "ability' together because they are so closely related. Talent means natural ability, skill, or aptitude, whereas ability alone has a stronger meaning, especially in the Greek. The word is "dunamis" and it means; "power, physical or moral, as residing in a person or thing; power in action." God has the ability (dunamis power) to heal the sick and perform miracles.

When you think of a talented person, you can understand that it's a power and a force in them. Of course, there must be care taken in wielding this power. If you let a child drive a powerful car, the results will often be destructive.

Power can become a god to some, and when that power is in the form of music, or any of the arts, (including speakers) it has the ability to hold the attention and even control others. This power, left unbroken by the Holy Spirit, will certainly corrupt.

If crowds of people come to see you perform your ability, they will see what God gave you. As long as God is acknowledged as the only One who should be praised for such a gift, there will be no idol worship. If that talent is offered to the god of "selfish ambition," or "self promotion," hiding as just a desire to please, it will be almost impossible for the audience not to be envious of you and your talent.

We all know what it feels like to desire another's talent, but the truth is we want the reaction to that talent more than the talent itself. Not many are willing to pay the price of developing the gifts God gives. (See the chapter called "Selling Your Talent.")

Levites in the Old Testament

> **And the Levites were numbered from thirty years old and upward, and their number by census of men was 38,000.**
>
> **Of these, 24,000 were to oversee the work of the house of the LORD; and 6,000 were officers and judges,**

and 4,000 were gatekeepers, and 4,000 were praising the LORD with the instruments which David made for giving praise (I Chronicles 23:3-5).

The musicians and singers were chosen by lot (see I Chronicles 25:8) to minister before the Lord. This means they drew straws to determine who would be in the band that praised the Lord. This also means they all had to qualify before the drawing. They were commanded by David to minister to the presence of God continually (see I Chronicles 16:37).

Only 4,000 were picked to minister in the Tabernacle on the instruments of music (see I Chronicles 23:5). This was done twenty-four hours a day. It is also believed that this lasted till the end of David's reign, which was thirty-three years. It continued into Solomon's temple, but it is not clear how long that lasted.

GOD CHOSE THE LEVITES

Long before David's time, the Lord chose the Levites to be His own. They were going to be a substitute or ransom for the first born of Israel.

And Jehovah spake unto Moses, saying,

And I, behold, I have taken the Levites from among the children of Israel instead of all the first-born that openeth the womb among the children of Israel; and the Levites shall be mine: (Numbers 3:11-12 ASV).

Thus shalt thou separate the Levites from among the children of Israel; and the Levites shall be mine.

And after that shall the Levites go in to do the service of the tent of meeting: and thou shalt cleanse them, and offer them for a wave-offering.

For they are wholly given unto me from among the children of Israel; instead of all that openeth the womb, even the first-born of all the children of Israel, have I taken them unto me (Numbers 8:14-16 ASV).

It is important for the Lord to choose who is going to serve Him or not. If a musician decides that he or she will be on the praise team without a clear call from God and the agreement of the leadership, then they will be self-appointed.

Self-appointment is very dangerous and will almost always lead to control and manipulation. (Remember the Pharisees were self-appointed.)

LEVITICAL HISTORY

If you are a musician or singer and believe that God has called you to be a modern day Levite, it may interest you to see a bit of their history.

1. The name Levi, means "A Joining."
2. Third son of Jacob and Leah (see Genesis 29:34).
3. Original ancestor of Israel's priests.
4. Levi was characterized in Scripture as savage and merciless. Levi, along with his brothers, while avenging the rape of their sister Dinah, annihilated the male population of the city of Shechem (see Genesis 34:25-31).
5. Jacob (his father) spoke harshly of Levi rather than blessing him (see Genesis 49:5-7).
6. The tribe that bears his name was also known as "instruments of wrath."
7. Moses ordered the Levites to kill all the people that had sinned by making the golden calf to worship. The Levites killed 3,000 men (brothers) that day (see Exodus 32:28).
8. Levites were the lowest of the three orders of Israel's priesthood.
9. Originally sacrifices were to be made by the first-born of each family. Later God chose the tribe of Levi to carry out this responsibility for Israel (see Numbers 3:12).

10. The tribe of Levi was chosen because they were the only tribe that stood with Moses when the people sinned by making a golden calf.

The Levites were not given an inheritance from the Promised Land. God was their inheritance.

"And to the sons of Levi, behold, I have given all the tithe in Israel for an inheritance, in return for their service which they perform, the service of the tent of meeting.

"And the sons of Israel shall not come near the tent of meeting again, lest they bear sin and die" (Numbers 18:21-22).

Only the sons of Aaron served as priests in Israel. Aaron was a Levite as was Moses, but there was a distinction as to who would be priest. Levites helped the priests carry out their duties and maintained the Tabernacle. They set up the Tabernacle and took it down when Israel moved. They camped around the Tabernacle when they did stop and their job was to protect it. There could be no layman or stranger coming near the Tabernacle or they would die (see Numbers 1:51).

NOTE: I believe the musicians in the church today should be spiritually camped around the Tabernacle to protect it. It is the musicians' job to stay alert during a praise time when the Spirit is moving. To put this in practical terms, not every person that comes to a Christian conference or special meeting is in love with Jesus. There is witchcraft and other demonic attempts to stop the people of God from praising His name. The higher praise goes, the more there will be attempts to stop it. The musicians and the leaders will usually have the discernment it takes to pick up on something like this and know how to pray against it.

They were also camped near in order to watch for the move of the Spirit. When the cloud began to move, the Levites were the first to notice and then they would take down the tent and follow. Israel followed thereafter. The Levite of today should be watching for the move of the Spirit and respond as soon as he sees it.

There is more on this in the chapter called "Practical Side of Praise."

DAVID INSTRUCTED THE MUSICIANS

And he (David) **appointed certain of the Levites to minister before the Ark of the Lord, and to record, and to thank and praise the Lord God of Israel (I Chronicles 16:4 KJV).**

"Record" meant that scribes or recorders would hear songs being offered to God in the Tabernacle and write them down. There are one hundred and fifty Psalms and they are broken up into groups. Songs of lament or complaint, thanksgiving, hymns that lift the congregation's praise to God, wisdom psalms, kingship ones, entrance ceremonies, teaching the expectations of God to His worshipers, enthronement psalms, songs of Zion, songs of confidence, prophetic ones, and liturgical psalms.

David was accredited with offering seventy-three songs to the book of Psalms. Asaph and his sons accounted for twelve, and twelve more by Korah and the sons of Korah along with two by Solomon, one by Ethan, and one by Moses. However, there are forty-nine that are anonymous. Others were written before the Tabernacle of David was built, some in the wilderness while he was fleeing from Saul, but many were recorded in the Tabernacle.

> NOTE: In our modern world "record" means something very different. I don't believe God is against recording praise in a studio or live, but I do believe the sales of these recordings cannot be the sole motivation for doing it. Scribes recorded the Psalms so that future generations would benefit from the level of praise, prophecy, and just plain realness that was expressed in these poems put to music. That should be a part of the motive today.

A VISION

Though there are no Scriptures that clearly define what the Tabernacle of David looked like, I believe it was an imitation of the Tent of Meeting that Moses built. I've wondered at times why David felt he had to build a new Tabernacle when the tent of Moses was still standing. This is where the Ark had been for many years and where Moses met with the God of Israel. However, the Tabernacle that Moses built is thought to have been moved to Nob, during Saul's reign, which was four miles away from Jerusalem. David fled there to see the priest Ahimelech when Saul wanted to kill him. The priests stayed at the Tabernacle, so it is assumed the tent was moved (see I Samuel 21:1).

I believe I saw what it might have looked like on the inside of the tent in a kind of vision. This is not a "thus sayeth the Lord," but an impression that helped me to better understand what must have happened in the Tabernacle of David.

The Tabernacle was dark because it was a tent with no windows. Little to no light from the day penetrated the inner court because the outer shell was three layers thick. There were lamp stands with candles burning and a continuous haze from the incense. The musicians were ministering continually and the presence of God was obviously strong though there is no mention in Scripture of the glory cloud being in David's tent, only in the Tent of Meeting and Solomon's temple. It must have been a dimly lit smoke-filled room with the sound of music and praise coming from all directions.

The musicians would band together in a half circle with their backs to anyone who came in the tent. They would face the veil that covered the Ark. There was space between the musicians so that anyone coming in would be able to see the veil and the view not be blocked by the musicians. (If you want to minister to God's people, then you must not block the view. God will make you transparent that He may be seen through you.)

David, or even someone from the city, would come into the Tabernacle late at night to cry out to God, and get caught up in the music and begin to offer a lament or a song of praise to God, and the recorders would scribe what they heard. The Psalms that are anonymous were offered by people the recorders didn't know, or it was too dark to see who was there. David's voice, or Asaph's and Korah's and their sons, were easy to recognize and their identity written with the Psalm.

When the musicians played a melody that was well-known and someone came in to offer praise, the melody or the lead instrument was sometimes mentioned along with the Psalm (see Psalm 61). That is where the instructions came from at the beginning of some Psalms. At the top of Psalm 62 there is mention of Juduthun, which most likely means the leader of the choir or even the recipient of the Psalm.

I know from playing with many veteran musicians over the years that whenever we played for a long time, it almost always completely spontaneous. I'm sure that these musicians could not have played the same songs every day without making some creative and spontaneous changes. In fact, I believe that it was the exception when the melody was recognizable by others, thus accounting for the mention of it in the heading of the Psalm. I'm convinced that rhythm patterns would get started and be played for hours when a spirit of intercession was there.

At times there would be a gathering of many people and David would begin singing a prophetic word to Israel or an exhortation calling the nations to praise God. Sometimes he would just shout of the mighty deeds of God and dance around like a wild man.

There is no reason to imagine that praise to God became sedate when the Ark was brought into the Tabernacle to stay. David told his wife, Michal, who objected to his wild dancing, that he would be yet more vile and base in his praise (see II Samuel 6:22). I cannot visualize what the praise was like after thirty-three years, but when Solomon finished the temple that David had a desire to build, the Glory of the Lord came in such a cloud that the priests could not stand to minister.

How much effect did the Levites' offering thanksgiving, praise, complaint, and prophecy, twenty-four hours a day, for thirty-three years, have on God's reaction to Solomon's sacrifice at the dedication of the Temple? I believe a lot. Furthermore, I believe that every day the Levites offered praise was a preparation for the thirty-three years that Jesus would walk the earth. Everything God does and every place He goes will always be preceded and followed with His praise. This is another reason for twenty-four-hour praise and intercession to become more of a reality.

Again, this is just a vision or insight of mine that helped me to better understand what the musicians were actually doing in the Tabernacle of David for thirty-three years. I also believe that the explanation of what really happened in there and what it felt like was deliberately left out of the Scriptures so we would not make a law or tradition around these events. What we can learn from David's experience is that God is not offended by a free expression of praise, or by our complaint, confession of sin, or prophetic proclamations to the people or the nations. He is also not afraid of the room being dimly lit or even trying to make some atmosphere inside of our places of worship.

With these examples of freedom staring back at us through the Psalms, why are we so afraid to express our true hearts to Jesus? It is in this hour that our true hearts will be revealed.

TRAINED TO PREPARE SACRIFICES

The Levites were trained in the art of preparing sacrifices so they would be acceptable to God. God is very clear on how He wanted offerings to be made to Him (see Leviticus laws).

That is still the case when the church comes together to make a sacrifice of praise. The job of the Levite in David's time was to lead praise when those sacrifices were being made. The job of the musician today is to lead praise while the people bring their praise offering to God. (Remember that the Hebrew root word for offering means to draw near.) The musicians need to be skilled enough to make that offering acceptable to God.

Please don't get confused between a musician that can play a lot of notes and one that is skillful. The Hebrew word for skillful that David used when instructing Chenaniah to teach the singers is the word "Biyn" (see I Chronicles 15:22). This word means to: "discern, understand, know (with the mind) to be cunning, distinguish, insight, discreet." Even the word *feel* is mentioned. For a praise leader to be right for the job, he must be able to read the hearts of God's people through discernment and even have a feel for what is happening. (There is more on this subject in the chapter "Worship Leader/ Transparent Man.")

If there is no understanding or discernment in the talented musician, then all you will have is someone who can play alot of notes. To discern the heart of God and then the heart of the people will require someone who has a relationship with the Father. That's what to look for in the musician with ability.

On the other hand, a musician must be showing signs of improvement continually, otherwise he or she is like the servant who buried his talent in the dirt. There must be a balance.

LEVITE OF TODAY

The work of the Levites made it possible for the people to come to the Tabernacle and make sacrifices for the atonement of sins. As a result of their work, the Holiness of the Tabernacle was maintained, and the glory of God remained with Israel.

I've got a list of duties they did and I want to show you some comparisons with today's "Levite." (Compare by looking at number 1 of "Levitical Duties Were" and number 1 of "Levites of Today" and so on.)

Levitical duties were:

1. Praise during sacrifices.
2. Preparing offerings.
3. Assisting the priests and carrying out their duties.
4. Keeping of the gates.
5. Judges.
6. Craftsmen.
7. Musicians.
8. Overseers of the royal treasury.
9. Teaching of the Scriptures to the people.

Levites of Today:

1. Sacrifice of praise.
2. Writing songs and knowing God's heart for the people in your church.
3. Assisting the leadership of your church. Knowing their heart and being an encouragement to them.

4. The place of praise in your church is the tabernacle of meeting, and the gates should be prayed over and anointed by the Levites regularly.
5. Judge means to contend and defend. The Levites should judge the spirit behind the songs that are offered. Judge when the Spirit wants to move or do something different today, and be a part of decisions made in the church.
6. A musician should be a craftsman, but I also believe that God is bringing artisans (carpenters, painters, potters, etc.) into the house of the Lord. They are Levites and as needed as any musician is.
7. Musicians.
8. This doesn't seem likely to happen, but there should be enough trust between the musician and leadership to get to this point.
9. A Levite should have enough knowledge of the Scriptures to teach at any time in the church or special meetings. They should be a constant reminder of the truth and the unshakable freedom given those who believe.

PREPARING FOR THE COMING WORKERS

The Scriptures tell us that a time is coming when the musicians and craftsmen will not be in the cities anymore.

And the voice of harpers and minstrels and flute-players and trumpeters shall be heard no more at all in thee; (Babylon) **and no craftsman, of whatsoever craft, shall be found any more at all in thee; and the voice of a mill shall be heard no more at all in thee; (Revelation 18:22 ASV).**

The name Babylon means "confusion or instability." This Scripture is saying that the creative people, the craftsmen, along with industry will be leaving the confusion and the instability of the marketplace. (When I looked up the word confusion, in many cases it meant shame, dishonor, or disappointed.)

Where do you think all these craftsmen and creative people are going to go when they leave the confusion of the workplace? They will go to the place where their craft is accepted. If that is the church, then we will all benefit from the change. If they go to the wilderness just to survive, then this opportunity to learn to love the stranger will pass by.

In Nehemiah 13:10 it says that the Levites and singers fled to their fields when Israel stopped giving their portion to them. The field is the workplace. We must pray that the ones He has called will respond to His voice, and when they do, I believe the provision will be there for them. Now is the time for the Levites in the church today to prepare for this. Jealousy will not get this job done. There must be enough discernment of spirits among the musicians to know when someone is operating out of a wrong spirit. The quality of everything to do with the church is going to rise up fast during this time. That rise is not for the purpose of making one church look better or bigger than another, but to show forth the glory of God that is around us. Being humbled by His mercy, yet boasting of His power.

ARE THERE REALLY LEVITES TODAY

> "Thus says the LORD, 'If you can break My covenant for the day, and My covenant for the night, so that day and night will not be at their appointed time,
>
> then My covenant may also be broken with David My servant that he shall not have a son to reign on his throne, and with the Levitical priests, My ministers.
>
> 'As the host of heaven cannot be counted, and the sand of the sea cannot be measured, so I will multiply the descendants of David My servant and the Levites who minister to Me'" (Jeremiah 33:20-22).

These Scriptures make it clear that there will be Levites serving before God for a long time. However, in the Old Testament the Levites were instructed by God to serve the priests in the work. In the New Testament things have changed as noted by Paul in his letter to the Hebrews.

> Now if perfection was through the Levitical priesthood (for on the basis of it the people received the Law), what further need was there for another priest to arise according to the order of Melchizedek, and not be designated according to the order of Aaron?
>
> For when the priesthood is changed, of necessity there takes place a change of law also.
>
> For the one concerning whom these things are spoken belongs to another tribe, from which no one has officiated at the altar.
>
> For it is evident that our Lord was descended from Judah, a tribe with reference to which Moses spoke nothing concerning priests.
>
> And this is clearer still, if another priest arises according to the likeness of Melchizedek,
>
> Who has become such not on the basis of a law of physical requirement, but according to the power of an indestructible life.
>
> For it is witnessed of Him "Thou art a priest forever according to the order of Melchizedek" (Hebrews 7:11-17).

Jesus is now the High Priest in the order of Melchizedek and He is from the tribe of Judah as was David. The Levites served David in his time and the Levites now serve Jesus. Being a musician doesn't make you a Levite, but being called to serve the Lord does. Gentiles are not descendants of the tribe of Levi, but through the blood of Jesus we are all adopted sons of the kingdom of God.

NEW TESTAMENT LEVITES

There are only two mentions of a Levite in the New Testament. One is a parable Jesus told in Luke 10:32, when a Levite passed by a man lying on the road, beaten and robbed; and the other is a Levite who sold everything he had to come and serve the disciples.

And Joseph, a Levite of Cyprian birth, who was also called Barnabas by the apostles (which translated means, Son of Encouragement),

And who owned a tract of land, sold it and brought the money and laid it at the apostles' feet (Acts 4:36-37).

These two examples of Levites reveal what the heart of today's musicians could be like. One Levite is looking out for himself, and the other is ready to sell it all for Jesus.

I think it is interesting that the only Levite mentioned by name in the New Testament is called "Son of Encouragement" and sold all he had to serve the purposes of Jesus. This Levite was making an example of heartfelt praise and worship to God, as was the history of his tribe.

It is also interesting to note, this is one verse away from the story of Ananias and Sapphira (see Acts 5:1) who held back some of their offering and died as a result.

If you want to be considered a Levite today, then lay what you have down at the feet of Jesus. Then you can serve His purposes not as an "Instrument of Wrath," but as a "Son of Encouragement." (Encouragement means a calling near, or a summons.)

The life of a Levite is still the same, even when his name is changed to Barnabas. The Levites called Israel to come near to God at Mount Sinai by playing the trumpet at the foot of the mountain. Moses was leading the multitudes (see Exodus 20:18). The musician/prophets who followed Samuel (see I Samuel 10), had an objective of calling the people back to God. The Levites prepared sacrifices before God which means drawing near.

Drawing near, calling others to come, and calling people back to God was the aim of a Levite then and is the same today.

chapter six
anointing

Anointing was the most unclear word I ever heard when I first got saved. I picked up right away that it was important to be anointed, and to use that anointing to minister, but it still remained a mystery. My first experience with it was when my wife and I were visiting a church in Nashville, Tennessee, named the House of Blessing. We were six months old in the Lord and a little afraid of being in a Spirit filled church. We had been warned about people that spoke in tongues, so I was on the lookout.

When we walked in the door, my wife began to weep. Since I had never had an experience with the power of the Holy Spirit, I didn't know what was happening to her. I was afraid someone would think I had been beating her.

We sat in the back in case we had to leave quickly. The sermon was on the prodigal son, of course, and a white haired man named Frank Gill walked through my life as he spoke. He couldn't have known me, I thought to myself, but somehow he's reading my mail. It was my first experience with someone walking in their anointing.

There we were, my wife still weeping from the presence of the Lord, and the people started singing in the Spirit—spontaneously. Never hearing anything like that before, I began to weep as I heard a multitude of singers joining in this praise.

As a humble man named Don Creech led the praise, I wept for ten minutes. I could not control my feelings. To my logical mind there was no real reason for me to cry, but my spirit-man was on fire from the experience. The anointing of God was just touching me. From that experience, I became addicted to the presence of the Lord.

ANOINTING OIL

Anointing oil was made by a perfumer (see Exodus 30:25), and was used to pour over the heads of those who were to come into the Presence of God. One had to be anointed to be a priest and serve in the Tent of the Lord. Objects that were to be in the Tabernacle had to be anointed to make them sacred. Moses, Aaron, and the sons of Aaron had to be anointed to fulfill the call on their lives.

For anyone to carry out a certain task unto the Lord, he had to be anointed to do it. The anointing empowered someone to walk it out. The Greek word "chrio" means: to anoint, consecrating Jesus to the Messianic office, and furnishing him with the necessary powers for its administration; enduing Christians with the gifts of the Holy Spirit.

When God touched my wife and me in that Nashville church, we were being anointed for the service of the Lord. There was no clear understanding of what that service was at that time, but I could play the guitar so we of course assumed that was the call. In a few years I found out that making that presumption was a mistake.

It's my belief that anyone who wants to walk out a life of service to God must first be touched by His anointing. This will begin an ongoing relationship with Him until you know what is on the heart of God. Many start out with a desire to please, not a desire to know. Jesus came that we might come to know God (see John 17:3). That anointing touch will draw you into wanting to know God.

What has God anointed you for and when is He going to start using you in that anointing? Before you answer that, let me show some of the things I found while trying to understand anointing better.

SAUL WAS ANOINTED TO BE KING

Saul was anointed by the prophet Samuel to be king of Israel. In I Samuel 9:2 there are some qualities attributed to Saul.

> **And he had a son, whose name was Saul, a choice young man, and a goodly: and there was not among the children of Israel a goodlier person than he: from his shoulders and upward he was higher than any of the people. (I Samuel 9:2 KJV).**

"**Goodly**" means well-pleasing, nice, pleasant, beautiful. Saul's qualities for being king were obvious to the eye. He was taller than anyone else.

Samuel told Saul in I Samuel 10:5 to go over to a place where he would be prophesied over by musician prophets. (There is more on the prophet/musicians in chapter 2.) And Saul would prophesy with them and be changed into another man. After Saul had gotten this information, he turned to go and the Lord did something to him that all of us could use. He changed his heart.

> **And it was so, that when he had turned his back to go from Samuel, God gave him another heart: and all those signs came to pass that day (I Samuel 10:9 KJV).**

God had to change Saul's mind-set in order to answer Israel's cry for a king. Saul was not born to be king; he had to be changed by God for that.

How many times have we put someone in a position of leadership in the church just because there was a need? Whenever man determines his own leader that has not been God's choice, man's choice will become the enemy of God's choice (i.e. Saul and David—Ishmael and Isaac).

ANOINTING WITH OR WITHOUT THE HOLY SPIRIT

I Samuel 16:14 says that the Spirit of the Lord departed from Saul. It doesn't say that his anointing left him. This verse also says that a tormenting spirit released by God came on him. Now there is a man with an anointing and a tormenting spirit. In I Samuel 16:16, Saul's servants are saying it's time to bring in a skillful or cunning musician to drive the tormenting spirit from Saul.

Was it David's skill or his anointing that drove the spirit away? Remember David was anointed to be the king not a musician.

Skill or cunning is the Hebrew word "yada," which means to know, or have an intimate knowing. David had an intimate knowing of music and an intimate knowing of God. Someone who really knows how to play an instrument and has an intimate relationship with God can have a powerful affect on others.

There's no Scripture prior to this that mentions demons leaving someone while a skillful musician plays. Saul's servants must have known something about this from past experience or they would have never made such a suggestion.

Impression: This is an impression I got one time while pondering all the events around Saul and David. I believe that a musician in David's time could not get formal training on an instrument other than experiential. Therefore, it was assumed by others that he must have had an encounter with God in order to play well: If a musician touched the heart of another simply by playing music, then it was believed the musician had a personal experience with God. This would explain why Saul's men suggested they find a skillful musician to relieve Saul of the tormenting demon.

This also explains why David required the Levites to study the Scriptures and to have played their instruments until they were thirty years old before qualifying to do Tabernacle duty. There are no Scriptures that I know of backing this idea, this is just an impression I have.

In spite of the fact that the demon left Saul when David played, it didn't last (see I Samuel 18:10). The demon got the best of Saul and he determined to kill David right in the middle of his playing one day. David, anointed, and the Holy Spirit upon him, became a target for the demonic.

A key to recognizing the anointing being activated in someone's life is being able to see the Spirit on him or her as well. Having an anointing to do something without the Holy Spirit will prove to be very frustrating as Saul's life gives testimony.

In Luke 4:18, Jesus is reading the Book of Isaiah in the synagogue, and the Scripture He reads says, **"The Spirit of the Lord is upon Me because He anointed Me to preach the gospel to the poor."** If the Spirit is not upon you, then wait for it, even if you are sure you know your appointed task.

Remember that before you can do the things you believe God has called you to, He must change your heart. That could happen in two minutes like it did with Saul, or take years like it did with David. David was anointed as a boy. Not until years later did he become king.

Before David became the king, he had all these qualities or talents in his life. As you look at the list, try to imagine what you would do with any of these attributes.

1. A skillful musician.
2. A mighty man of valor.
3. A warrior.
4. One prudent in speech.
5. Handsome man.
6. The Lord is with him (see I Samuel 16: 18).

This doesn't even mention that he was a shepherd that fought a bear and a lion to protect the sheep he watched over. God was choosing the right man to watch over His people.

These qualities could have easily been used for a number of things to benefit David's life. Many men would give everything to have just some of these qualities.

All of these talents were a part of David's life as God's plan to make him ready to be king. There is no mention of David having leadership qualities, nor Scriptures that tell of David being trained for ruling Israel. The point is, *God only anointed David to be king*. He did not anoint him to be a musician or a warrior. He didn't anoint him to be a man of valor or prudent in speech.

This should serve as a warning to those who have attributes like David. Trying to take advantage of qualities that come natural to you can be the distraction that keeps you from walking in your true anointing.

TALENTS ARE USEFUL

After David became king all these qualities became useful to him. His skill as a musician and psalmist helped form the entire idea of worshiping God in Spirit and in truth. His valor caused him to be courageous in battle. His ability to war was not only translated to the battlefield, but also in the playing of the instrument. Being prudent in speech made it possible for him to communicate well with the people he led.

Today, if someone had all these qualities, we would say they had "charisma." *Webster's Dictionary* has a revealing definition for this word: "gift of God's grace or talent; a special quality of leadership that captures the popular imaginations and inspires unswerving allegiance and devotion."

In spite of the fact "charisma" is the Greek word for anointing; the Greek definition says nothing about a quality of leadership that causes others to follow. Though we would all like to have charisma (the English version that is), it is not what it means to be anointed.

This is why Jesus had no stately form to be attracted to (see Isaiah 53:2). Our worship of Him must be from a spiritual revelation, not an attraction to comeliness or the English translation of charisma. This is a very important issue as it pertains to discerning the anointing on someone's life. Because a musician has charisma doesn't automatically mean he is anointed.

QUESTION

Do you really know what God has anointed you for? Are you confused about what to do in ministry because you have this talent that seems to be very useful to others? Have others encouraged you to do something with your talent, and you are now trying to fulfill their dream? If this is happening or has happened to you, get free as quickly as you can. Then ask the Lord to show you His plan for you and the talents He gave you.

PAUL ANOINTED FOR GENTILES

The Apostle Paul was a Jew through and through. He called himself a Pharisee of Pharisees. He was indeed the right man for the job. All of his natural life and upbringing was just right for ministering to the Jews. Yet God anointed him for the Gentiles (see Acts 13:44).

Peter was anointed to minister to the Jews, yet he was a simple fisherman. I would have chosen Paul for the Jews and Peter for the Gentiles, but God didn't. This only serves to prove that we are not the best judges of what use God has planned for the anointing in our lives.

IS EVERYONE ANOINTED?

We are all anointed to know the truth. Knowing the truth will set us free.

> **But you have an anointing from the Holy One, and all of you know the truth (I John 2:20 NIV).**
>
> **As for you, the anointing you received from him remains in you, and you do not need anyone to teach you. But as his anointing teaches you about all things and as that anointing is real, not counterfeit-just as it has taught you, remain in him (I John 2:27 NIV).**

This doesn't mean there will be no more teachers, but that when you do hear the Word, the anointing will cause you to understand.

I feel there is some misunderstanding about the word "anointing." It is customary, in Charismatic circles, to say someone is anointed when we really mean "I feel the presence of the Lord." If the people feel His presence when praise starts, they will sometimes say, "That was anointed praise." The truth is, people are feeling the presence of the "anointed One."

WARNING

Jesus gives us a warning about people coming in His name and saying they are Christ. As you read Matthew 24:4-5 remember Christ means "anointed."

> **And Jesus answered and said unto them, "Take heed that no man deceive you.**
>
> **"For many shall come in my name, saying, I am Christ; and shall deceive many"** (KJV).

Three Gospels use the same wording, **"I am Christ"** instead of "I am the Christ" (see also Mark 13:6, Luke 21:8). It is seldom a coincidence when three writers use the same words. There is a point the Lord is making here. When this Scripture is preached, it's usually translated "beware of someone who calls himself the Savior, or Christ Himself." However, I believe the Lord is revealing a subtle difference between someone saying he is the Christ, compared to someone saying he is anointed. It is hard to imagine anyone actually calling himself the resurrected Christ returned, but it's not so hard to imagine someone proclaiming they are anointed.

"Deceive" means: "to lead astray or to sever or fall away from the truth." Have you ever known the anointing on someone to lead others astray or cause them to wander from the truth? There are a few rock artists that have an anointing on their lives and they are leading our young people astray with that anointing. Remember, the gifts and callings are without repentance (see Romans 11:29). The same Greek word is used for gifts and anointing.

If someone sees an anointing on you and speaks it to you, graciously thank them and wait for the Lord to bring it to pass. If it is truly there, God won't take it away from you if you don't try to make it happen. The effort to fulfill that kind of word in the natural will spiritually deaden most people. The idea of telling others that you are anointed has a measure of pride in it and that will always precede a fall (see Proverbs 16:18). If a person has spoken an untrue word about you being anointed, and you pursue what *they* believe is true, you will be in error and will spend a lot of time trying to get back on track.

This warning from Jesus says much more than to be on the lookout for a false Christ. This is an encouragement for all to wait on the Lord and His anointing to be revealed in us, then waiting for the Holy Spirit to activate that anointing (see Luke 4:18).

BURDEN OF THE SONG

Have you ever felt like leading praise week after week was sometimes more of a burden than a blessing? Many Sundays I would leave church struggling to stay awake long enough to get home and take a nap. Praise seemed to weigh a ton and it was all on my shoulders. Now I realize it is true; there is a burden involved with praise. Just not the way I first thought. Let me explain.

In I Chronicles 15:22 instructions are being given to the Levites.

And Chenaniah, chief of the Levites, was for song: he instructed about the song, because he was skillful (KJV).

"Instruct" is a very strong word here. It means to chastise (with blows) or figuratively (with words). That doesn't sound like a class in songwriting where everyone gets a chance to try a song out on the congregation. It was very strong instruction and there is a reason.

The Hebrew word "messa" is used for the word "song." It means: "a burden, lifting a load, a tribute, what is carried or brought or borne." The reason the instructions in song were so strong was because the songs were carrying a burden. They weren't just writing songs to the Lord, they were carrying His presence. Look at I Chronicles 15:26.

And it came to pass, when God helped the Levites that bare the ark of the covenant of the LORD, that they offered seven bullocks and seven rams (KJV).

When the Lord helps by the anointing to carry the burden of His own presence, then a true sacrifice can be realized. Without the help of the Lord, the Levites could not have made the sacrifices necessary to draw near to God. The same must happen when leading praise. If the Lord is not helping your song carry the burden of His presence with the anointing, then the sacrifice part of a "sacrifice of praise" will not be realized (see Hebrews 13:15). The song carries the burden as we make the sacrifice. The weight of His presence is too great for anyone to carry without the anointing. That is why it feels so bad when there is no anointing during a praise session. It is because the leader is trying to offer God a ride on a vehicle (song) that is not capable of carrying His presence. When His presence does come, He has to help carry the load anyway. So there must be understanding in the songs that are offered to God or you won't get His help carrying the presence (read the story of David trying to bring the Ark back into Jerusalem on an ox cart, I Chronicles 13:7 and following).

There were times when leading week after week I would just sing the song that I thought would please the people the most. Perhaps a song that always seemed to get them dancing, or the one the pastor said was anointed. At that point, I was no longer listening to the Sprit; I was only doing what I knew would please men. This is why I was going home exhausted on Sunday. I was carrying the burden of the church and not the burden of the Lord, which He would help me carry. When I did learn to carry His burden and not the church, I never went home tired again.

There is something else very interesting in I Chronicles 15:15: **And the children of the Levites bare the ark of God upon their shoulders with the staves thereon, as Moses commanded according to the word of the Lord (KJV).** The term **"The children of the Levites"** means the offspring of the Levites. It is the sons or the young ones that will be carrying the burden.

Right now young people are starting to carry a burden in their hearts for God. This is fast turning into a revival among the youth. They are the ones that will carry this burden, but if the fathers do not do their part, it will be short-lived. The priests made sacrifices so the songs could carry the burden. With God helping them to carry the presence and the fathers making sacrifices of prayer, praise, and intercession for the youth, there will come a lasting revival.

A song to the Lord must be done a certain way—skillfully. That word strikes fear in the hearts of many a writer, but it shouldn't. At the end of I Chronicles 15:22 it says, **"because he was skillful."** That is the Hebrew word biyn (bene); it means: "understanding: to be cunning diligent, direct, discerning eloquent, feel, have intelligence, to know." Skillful really means to know music and have a feel for it. That doesn't mean playing a lot of notes, but to really know something. David played with this kind of knowing and it drove demons away from Saul.

I know there could be lengthy conversations on the subject of skill in a praise leader and the musicians in the church. Not all churches have what the world calls skillful musicians available to them. So they do with the best they have. Offering your best to God is the bottom line. The level of raw talent in every musician varies so there can be no criteria for what is considered skillful: only heart and understanding. We are all capable of understanding if we ask of the Lord, and we are all able to have a feel or heart for music. (There is more on this in the chapter called, "The Practical Side of Praise".)

I've heard it said on many occasions that some very limited musicians were leading praise and the presence of the Lord fell very strong in the church. The argument is that it doesn't take a great musician for God to manifest His Spirit at a gathering.

This is very true. God meets the hunger of His people at any gathering. Whenever God-starved people come together, they will experience His presence with or without music. Also, the presence of the Spirit comes in waves as it does in heaven.

It's when we are at a low point that a good musician comes in handy. His understanding, skill, and feel for music will keep the enemy from inciting anxiousness and that "let's take over and save the service" spirit that comes on the people when the musicians don't know what to do next. When the anointing is strong, a decent whistler can lead praise.

On the other hand, a great musician that overplays for the sake of proving his worth can actually invite demons to the stage. (The opposite of David playing with true skill and Saul being freed from demons.) Strife, envy, and competition to name a few, will come boldly on stage with the musicians if this is what good players are doing. The gifted musician must be broken and humbled under the mighty hand of God before he or she can be used to carry the burden of His presence. It is not the job of another to break a musician, but he must humble himself.

God must be the helper of the praise leader to carry His presence and to accomplish His purpose in a time of sacrifice. All other ways are strife.

Riding the Anointing

Another aspect of the anointing that has been overlooked is riding on it. I listened to a young praise leader on a tape someone gave me. She was anointed, but the band playing with her just rode on her gift. I could hear her straining under the extra burden of not only carrying the presence of the Lord, but also carrying the band. At the end of the session she must have been exhausted. I'm sure she was not aware of carrying the band as she had done that very thing many times before.

At several points during the session, other members would try to take over the lead from her. It sometimes sounded like they were trying to help or just encourage, but what they did never seemed to help or support her. I knew this band from an earlier experience I had with them, and it was common for them to look for an opportunity to take over the lead. Right then the Lord showed me the difference between the song carrying the burden of His presence with God helping, and the anointing trying to carry the band and sometimes the church as well, and God NOT helping.

The band is supposed to carry their part of the burden, not be a part of the load. I'm sure this band thought they were serving the leader by helping her lead. Some like to refer to this as "moving freely in the Spirit" That type of freedom is more license than liberty.

I can hear arguments as I write, so let me try to better explain what I mean. Only listening to the Spirit should give a backup musician the divine timing needed to play at the right time, lay out when necessary, etc.

Imagine for a moment, that playing in the praise band is like the Levites carrying the Ark on their shoulders. The guys in the back must follow the guys in the front or the Ark will fall when disunion starts. If the guys in the back decide to lie on the

Ark, the leader will have to drag the whole mess along the road. This doesn't mean the leader is making all the right choices, it just means they are the leader.

In practical terms, this means musicians who are limited players and show no desire to improve, yet insist on playing a large role on every song, are in effect taking over the lead. This applies to singers as well. Another example is musicians who have personal agendas and just wait for someone with an anointing to carry them closer to it, or good players who make judgments about other musicians based solely on their own criteria and not the anointing.

These are only a few examples of what I've heard over the years, not to mention all the great times I've had with musicians who do play with sensitivity and are determined to support. The examples I'm making are only to show how much extra burden there can be on a praise leader if there aren't some clear guidelines. If you are a limited musician and you know it, stay out of the way when a song you don't know comes along. Do all your experimenting at home and not before God Almighty.

If you are rehearsing the compliments you've heard and not your instrument, it's time to take those thoughts captive.

chapter seven
entertainment

Entertainment is almost a dirty word in the church, and yet there is a good bit of it there. After being an entertainer for many years before salvation, I find that entertainment has gotten a bad rap in some cases and is running wild in others.

After some study I found some interesting information about this phenomenon that holds the hearts of many Americans.

Webster's Dictionary has a definition for entertainment that describes it as a distraction or diversion from your daily life. The Bible explains entertainments as "feasts," that were sometimes connected with a public festival and accompanied by offerings. An entertainment was in connection with domestic or social events, as at the weaning of children or a wedding. The guests were invited by servants who assigned them their respective places. Like portions were sent by the master to each guest except when special honor was intended.

The Israelites were forbidden to attend heathenish sacrificial entertainments (see Exodus 34:15), because these were in honor of false gods, and because at such feasts they would be liable to partake of unclean flesh (see I Corinthians 10:28). In the entertainments common in apostolic times among the Gentiles were frequent "reveling," against which Christians were warned (see Romans 13:13; Galatians 5:21; I Peter 4:3, *Easton's Bible Dictionary*).

The major reason the Jews were warned against the entertainments of the Gentiles was not because the gifted performers would pervert them, but because they might partake of the sacrifice that was made to false gods. This is like learning good principles from a humanistic or new age book. The principles will draw you to read, but somewhere in it is a sacrifice to a false god. (Remember, sacrifice means "drawing near.")

Using gifted entertainers to get the attention of the public is a common practice. I am not speaking against that business or the idea of using music or talented people for the sale of a product. The Christian music business or Christian entertainment business came from the idea of a believer needing a safe way to go to a show or buy a CD without worrying about a tribute or sacrifice being made to a false god sometime during the performance. However, there is a big difference between Christian entertainment and praise to the Most High.

In the life of a gifted musician, singer, or generally creative person, there may be a call to give all they have for the purpose of praising God and Him alone. This can happen early in one's creative life, but mostly I find the call happening after some experience, training, and anointing is clearly seen in their lives.

Sometimes the Lord uses the world as a training ground for the gifted person, even if they are believers. Sometimes He uses the church to train them and then sends them to the world. In whatever pattern the Lord prefers to use, you must obey His call.

JUDGMENT IN THE THEATER

Have you ever felt judged when leading praise or even when you stand up to make announcements in the church? Sometimes you feel like you must have forgotten to put all of your clothes on before you left for church and everyone is looking at your bare spot. There is a reason for feeling that way—people are judging. They are judging because we all feel as though we are called to judge everything that enters a stage. Let me show you what I mean.

The word theater is mentioned in Acts 19:29-31. To the Jews, the theater was a place for judgment or worship. It was where the elders would come together to judge a matter. Praise was sometimes done in this place as well. Now look at the Greek definition of this word.

Theater: "a place for public show; a spectacle."

Public drama was apparently unknown in Old Testament Israel except for possible worship activities and only arrived with the Greeks after 400 B.C. Herod I built numerous theaters in Palestine (37-4 B.C.). This infuriated the Jews when there was a theater built near the Temple in Jerusalem. Outside of Israel, theaters were abundant and they were used for public performances that began with sacrifices to pagan deity: the patron god of that city. Dramas and comedies were political and historical in content and often were lewd and suggestive. This is why the Jews were forbidden to go to such activities. (Source, *Holman Bible Dictionary.*)

From the forced marriage of these two cultures, the Jew judging and sometimes worshiping in the theater, and the Greek entertaining with spectacle in the theater, there emerged a third culture. People began to go to the theater to judge entertainment. It wasn't long before judging praise became a part of the culture, too. That is why modern Christians feel they must judge or grade the praise in their churches.

I have been both over-commended and criticized for leading praise. It's like shouting out the window at your car in the driveway saying, "I love the way you carry me to work," or "you're stupid, you're a terrible ride." A praise leader is a vehicle and praise is a road we travel to meet with our King.

If your car fails to take you to work enough times, you get another car. If it does succeed at this task, then take care of it and do some preventative work now and again. Praise is like the car you use for work. It is not a luxury item; it is a necessity. You won't make it in life if you fail to get to work enough times, and you won't make it in the Spirit and in life if you don't make it to the presence of God.

Don't get the wrong impression here. When I'm leading, I like it when someone feels the presence of the Lord, and I don't mind hearing that afterwards. However, it is the presence that I need to be concerned about, rather than whether this session was as high as the one we had a month ago when everyone was on the floor.

There are times when I say to my wife, "I love you," and it has great impact on her. There are other times when it doesn't visibly move her at all. If I had someone sitting out there in the theater of life yelling, "there's not enough fire on the way you say, 'I love you,'" I would come under that judgment and eventually start to perform for that critic.

TV Theater

The theater that we most regularly attend today is television. Armed with a remote control, we sit in the judgment seat and adjudicate in seconds as we search for something that will stand out to us. Unconsciously we learn to pass judgment instantly on every picture and every sound without as much as a blink of an eye. It is not hard to imagine why we pass judgment on praise and preaching. It is this scenario that causes musicians and speakers to begin to perform for their congregations.

I'm not speaking against performing in a theater, or expressing yourself through your gift in front of others. There are few things in the world of art that are more wonderful than live theater done well. A rock band really learning how to have a good time in music, or a bluegrass band set up on a lawn somewhere and all those gathered around, dancing, and fully enjoying this impromptu event. I speak nothing against the spontaneous life of the truly creative, only concern about using entertainment (which means distraction) in the church to lull a congregation into a routine.

> **But ye are a chosen generation, a royal priesthood, an holy nation, a peculiar people; that ye should shew forth the praises of him who hath called you out of darkness into his marvelous light: (I Peter 2:9 KJV).**

In the final analysis, we *are* supposed to put on a show—a showing forth of His praises. That is because we are called out of the darkness.

The world and the critics of the church will always judge the people of God and a move of the Spirit. That judgment might as well be because we are dancing and praising the Lord. Fear of man may be the strongest weapon the devil has against the church. If we let that fear turn us into performers of praise or preaching, we will lead God's children astray.

DANCE/PROPHETIC INTERCESSION

The Greeks also introduced dance as entertainment. Again the children of Israel had a completely different purpose for this kind of movement. Dance was another way the Jews expressed worship. They danced for joy, prophetically, and in intercession.

Dance is quite innocent when used most places in Scripture, such as: **"Then shall the virgin rejoice in the dance, both young men and old together..." (Jeremiah 31:13 KJV).**

The King James uses the word **"dance"** eight times in the Bible.

Most of the time it means spinning around, skipping, and leaping for joy. However, there is one time in Judges that dance takes on a new meaning.

And see, and, behold, if the daughters of Shiloh come out to dance in dances, then come ye out of the vineyards, and catch you every man his wife of the daughters of Shiloh, and go to the land of Benjamin (Judges 21:21 KJV).

This time the word dance is the Hebrew word "chuwl", and it means: "to twist, fear, tremble, be in anguish, whirl about (in travail with), bear, dance, bring forth, to drive away, to wait anxiously, to be made to writhe, to be born, suffering torture (participle) to wait longingly, to be distressed."

Have you seen this kind of thing happen in your church or in a conference? I've seen people tremble before the Lord, and travail and even look like they are giving birth. I have also seen many offended by this and others trying to make excuses for such actions. What is happening (mostly to women) is nothing new. Let me show you.

The dance that the women did at all the feasts of Israel is explained in Judges. Though the word dance is used in Scripture many times, in this one incident the author uses the word "chuwl".

I have tried to visualize this, but it is hard to imagine just what these dances really looked like. If the men from Benjamin found it easy to steal the women during the dance, then what kind of dance was this? If we look at the history of the Jews, and the reason God commanded them to have these feasts, there may be an answer.

Since the Jews were not big on entertainment, and God commanded them to re-enact the victories He had won for them, then this was a visual record of a kind of the historical events that shaped Israel. This also explains why the festival dance is defined as travail, or birthing.

I've said all this to say, I believe the dance before the Lord has more than one purpose. We are expected and commanded to dance before the Lord. Sometimes that dance is a joyful time of leaping and skipping about. Other times it is a re-enactment of the battles God has fought on our behalf.

Psalm 149:3 says, **"Let them praise his name in the dance"** (KJV), the root word for dance is chuwl. The psalmist is encouraging Israel to dance like the dances done at the feasts before the Lord.

What does a prophetic dance or movement look like? What would an enactment of the victories of Jesus look like? I don't think this could be defined in words, but I believe the definition of chuwl becomes clearer as I ponder this.

When looking at the Hebrew word for intercession (paga: "to encounter, to push against, to rush at someone with hostile violence, to strike or hit the mark"), you can see that the above mentioned kind of dance looked like a physical expression of their intercession.

All this changed when the Greeks introduced dance as an expression of sensuality and lust. From the initiation of lewdness in the dance, it wouldn't be long before the Hebrew tradition of prophetic movement took on a fear of sensuality.

The mix of travailing in birth with sensuality would cause a stir indeed among those just learning to walk in holiness.

Dance was outlawed in the early Christian church because of the Greek influence on it. A woman whirling around with an expression of anguish and travail as if in childbirth would be pretty unnerving for anyone who hadn't seen something like that before. What was once dance intercession and expressions of joy for the God of Israel was now seen as lewd and suggestive.

I know that I have only touched the surface of the purposes of dance, but I feel the entire subject of prophetic movement and dance intercession has just begun. It will take some time to see where God wants to go with this awesome expression.

Someone once said of my wife, who is inspired in prophetic movement, "she is like the leaves of a tree. They respond to the slightest breeze before the branches feel the power of the wind." This kind of response to the wind of the Spirit will require a selfless person and a real understanding of the things of the Lord. There can be no entertainment or judgment of the things of the Spirit.

Selfish Ambition

Today the entertainment business is one of the strongest forces on the earth, and it brings a spirit with it—SELFISH AMBITION. **"Do nothing out of selfish ambition or vain conceit, but in humility consider others better than yourselves" (Philippians 2:3 NIV).**

To be a successful entertainer in the world, you must consider yourself the best and disregard others. You won't get any work if you hold someone else in higher regard than yourself. However, there are consequences for embracing selfish ambition.

> **But if you have bitter jealousy and selfish ambition in your heart, do not be arrogant and {so} lie against the truth.**
>
> **This wisdom is not that which comes down from above, but is earthly, natural, demonic.**

For where jealousy and selfish ambition exist, there is disorder and every evil thing (James 3:14-16).

Arthur Burt writes in his book *Surrender*, "What a man believes, rules him! He does not rule what he believes." If you believe you were meant to be a star or an entertainer on stage, that will rule you. If you believe you want to be Christ-like, then it is time to humble yourself. It is completely possible to be an entertainer and humble yourself at the same time, but that will only be a holy thing if you surrender to the Lord.

chapter eight
talent for sale

Have you ever met someone whose presence was able to light up a room? Even though you are meeting them for the first time, you feel as though you've known them all your life. They carry conversations when everyone else is too cautious to talk. Kids are often attracted to them and everyone seems to know them, or wishes they did. Such people are typically the life of the party, but their outgoing personalities can get them into trouble now and again.

Believe it or not, this is a talent from God. We sometimes call it "charisma." Not to be confused with the "charisma" or "anointing" referred to in the Bible in connection with supernatural gifts and manifestations of the Holy Spirit.

This type of human charisma, as I mentioned in an earlier chapter, is defined in *Webster's Dictionary* as "a gift of God's grace; a divinely inspired gift or talent; to rejoice at. A special quality of leadership that captures the popular imaginations and inspires unswerving allegiance and devotion."

When this gift is put together with some kind of talent including music, the arts, or speaking ability, you have a celebrity. If such people are not yet well-known, they have only to try a little and they usually succeed at gaining acclaim.

Before you think I'm describing something sinful, I want to show you a Hebrew word in the Bible that has a similar definition to charisma. It's the word HALAL. It's one of the seven Hebrew words for praise I mentioned earlier. It means: "to be bright; to shine, to be splendid; to boast, to be praised;" it even includes to be famous in the definition. (Keep in mind that the Hebrew uses the word famous as one with a good name or someone called out by name.)

Although charisma describes an alluring quality, halal seems to be more of the achievement of that quality. You might say charisma is the baby and halal is the adult. There is a warning in Scripture about dealing or using this God-given gift foolishly.

> I (God) **said unto the fools, Deal not foolishly: and to the wicked, Lift not up the horn:**
>
> **Lift not up your horn on high: speak not with a stiff neck.**
>
> **For promotion cometh neither from the east, nor from the west, nor from the south.**
>
> **But God is the judge: he putteth down one, and setteth up another (Psalm 75:4-7 KJV).**

The words **"fools"** and **"foolishly"** in verse 4 are both translated halal. The word fool is never mentioned in that word's definition, so how did fool get translated halal? All this caught my interest so I started looking a little closer at what the Lord might be saying in the strange use of this word.

HISTORY OF THE FOOL

In times long past, the word "fool" was used to refer to an entertainer. The fool was kept in the house of a nobleman or king to entertain by joking or clowning. The subjects of the nobleman would always search the land over for the best of the fools and offer them to their master in hopes of bringing pleasure to him. The best of the entertainers would light up the room when they walked in, and if the king was pleased all the people in the land were blessed. The pleasure of the king was all that was important. Of course, a fool could lose his head if he didn't please the king. It has a way of really sharpening your act.

It wasn't long before the entertainer, or fool, started turning his attention to trying to please the people of the court, instead of just pleasing the king. In fact some fools abandoned the objective of entertaining the king altogether, deeming it too risky. There was less reward entertaining outside the court, but you could keep your head if you weren't very talented.

The problem with trying to please the crowd instead of the king was there were as many opinions of what was good as there were people in the crowd. No one could possibly please everyone. Yet, many fools never realized that it would be easier to just try and please the king, than to continually be reshaping one's self to fit the fickle demands of the public.

The outcome of this situation was probably predictable. In order to entertain the people and hang on to your head, a fool needed to learn how to *sell himself*. This is the very place that many entertainers and even worship leaders find themselves in today.

When I worked as a studio musician it was a good idea to promote yourself if you wanted another job in the future with that artist or producer. Of course, I was too humble to actually promote myself so I would tell the artist what they really needed for their career was a guitar player who had a guitar just like mine. And someone who plays just like I do. By the time I was finished I had convinced them they just needed to hire me to solve all their recording needs. Oh I thought I was being very subtle, but it was self-promotion. In spite of the fact I thought myself too humble to openly promote, I did just that on every session. The Lord had to convict me before I saw what a trap this was. He would do that by making my voice sound like a TV announcer. In my head my voice sounded so unreal that I would stop in mid-sentence and say to myself; "Who is this phony talking?" It wasn't long before I couldn't get away with this kind of obvious devaluing of His gift to me. Only God can truly promote.

Psalm 75:4 could be paraphrased like this: "to the bright and shining people that are very good at what they do, beware of the temptation to sell yourself and your talent." The end of that verse says, **"and to the wicked, Lift not up the horn."** Horn means power. Do not lift up or exalt the power of the wicked.

Many times someone who has great power and wealth is admired and held in high esteem, even when they have questionable character and are sometimes just wicked men. For sure, a powerful person can get away with being just a little off with no objections at all.

The *Hebrew Lexicon* makes an interesting statement concerning the meaning of wicked. It says, "People with this characteristic are guilty of violating the social rights of others through oppression, greed, exploitation, murder, dishonesty in business, and twisting justice."

It is against God to exalt any man on the basis of his wealth, influence, or power, especially if he is wicked.

There are several other verses in Psalm 75 that have a bearing on this matter of selling your talent:

> **Lift not up your horn on high: speak not with a stiff neck.**
>
> **For promotion cometh neither from the east, nor from the west, nor from the south.**
>
> **But God is the judge: he putteth down one, and setteth up another (Psalm 75:5-7 KJV).**

Don't promote yourself, even if you feel you have the greatest gift in the history of mankind. Only God's favor matters, and He is quite capable of promoting you if He wants to. The scriptural route to promotion is actually very clear: **"Humble yourselves in the sight of the Lord, and he shall lift you up" (James 4:10 KJV).** The hard part is waiting for God to lift you up. If you are unwilling or unable to wait, the consequences will not be promotion but abasement.

WHAT IF YOU'RE ALREADY FAMOUS?

If you have already promoted yourself into a position of recognition and feel as though you can't back out now, think again. Even though you might be on your way to being something really great in music or in ministry, stop and consider the lessons we saw in the history of the fool. Pleasing the King is all that really matters. If God is not the One who has promoted you—or if He did promote you and it is now out of control—stop everything and seek the Lord. Your life and ministry will be in the balance.

I spoke with Jim Bakker one time after he had been released from prison. Among the many words of wisdom he spoke, one thing stood out to me. He said there was a time in the beginning of his ministry when he was questioning if God was in some of the things that were happening. But because it was growing so fast, and there was so much good being done as a result, no one would let him stop. He couldn't imagine letting all those people down. He was caught in a ministry machine that had started running itself. The approval of the King had become secondary to the approval of the crowd.

This is an terrible trap. Only a few have made it out of such a place without offending many people. But pleasing or upsetting people is not what's important. Pleasing God is.

When you get out of bed tomorrow morning, ask yourself this question: Whose "fool" will I be today, the King's or the crowd's?

Jesus said it this way: **"For unto whomsoever much is given, of him shall be much required: and to whom men have committed much, of him they will ask the more" (Luke 12:48 KJV).**

I've heard this Scripture quoted many times, but only the first half of it. It seems to always be used to make a gifted person feel like he or she owes God something that can only be paid by using the gift in ministry. It's the second half that caught my attention. This Scripture is saying that if I commit much to man, whether in ministry or in a worldly occupation, man will ask of me even more than what I've committed. Haven't you found that in your own life? The job always seems to grow as you get further along. God, on the other hand, will only require what He has given. Not more than I have, but the same as I have. Many times I've been too overwhelmed by commitments I've made to man to be available to God. It's no wonder Jesus says, **"My yoke is** easy" (see Matthew 11:30). It's man's yoke that kills. (I mention this Luke 12:48 Scripture a few times in this book. I think it's a point that cannot be over-emphasized.)

MEANT FOR WORSHIP

As already stated the word halal is a word mostly used in the Old Testament for praise. Halal is exemplified by God Himself. He is bright, shining, praiseworthy, and causes the things around Him to shine. In the *Hebrew Lexicon*, it also mentions that some people can have a halal quality, though not at the level God has it. It's interesting to note the people who were considered halal in the Bible.

In Genesis 12:15, Pharaoh's men were praising (halal) Sarai for her beauty. Sarai's beauty stemmed from a godly attractiveness in her life, and all who met her recognized it.

Of Absalom, David's son, it was said, **"In all Israel there was not a man so highly praised for his handsome appearance as Absalom" (II Samuel 14:25 NIV).** Though he was handsome and bright, Absalom believed his favor and gifts were greater than his duty to honor his father.

Esther was considered to have had a halal quality. Both Esther and Vashti were beautiful, but it was not spoken of Vashti to have been halal. When she refused the king's request to come to him, she lost her position of favor. Without godly character and the fear of the Lord, this great ability is destined to go the way of Absalom and Vashti. Esther, on the other hand, had a different testimony: **"And Esther obtained favour in the sight of all them that looked upon her" (Esther 2:15 KJV).**

This same kind of favor is found in the Proverbs 31:10-31 description of a virtuous woman: **"Many women do noble things, but you surpass them all. Charm is deceptive, and beauty is fleeting; but a woman who fears the LORD is to be praised.** (Halal) **Give her the reward she has earned, and let her works bring her praise** (halal) **at the city gate" (Proverbs 31:29-31 NIV).**

Again, halal is used to describe a God-given charisma that either can be used by Him for His glory, or perverted into something we use for our selfish ends.

Halal is not a praise that we should seek for ourselves, but rather it is a praise that comes naturally to those who radiate the presence and character of Christ. And it is important to see that halal is much more than a matter of being born with an optimistic personality. All who have an intimate relationship with the Lord can be radiant in His presence.

"Everyone Says I Should Do Something With My Talent"

Over the years I've heard many people tell me "everyone says I should try to do something with my talent." My response often surprises them: If you are trying to do something with your talent simply because everyone else is telling you to, you will miss the timing of God and possibly fail to notice your call altogether. God must be your promoter and you must rely on His management skills.

"Ministry" can be just as seductive as the lure of secular fame. If someone is telling you that you should be ministering to the people with your talent, be careful. Well-meaning friends should only be confirming what you already know from God.

When you've dreamed for years of singing in public or serving God with your talent, it's hard to imagine not promoting yourself to fulfill that dream. Many feel the best way to serve God is to become well-known and reach as many people as possible. It's a good idea except for one thing—the Word.

> **But God hath chosen the foolish things of the world to confound the wise; and God hath chosen the weak things of the world to confound the things which are mighty;**
>
> **And base things of the world, and things which are despised, hath God chosen, yea, and things which are not, to bring to naught things that are:**

That no flesh should glory in his presence.

But of him are ye in Christ Jesus, who of God is made unto us wisdom, and righteousness, and sanctification, and redemption:

That, according as it is written, He that glorieth, let him glory in the Lord (I Corinthians 1:27-31 KJV).

A friend once told me the story of a young girl who had a wonderful singing voice. She tried to get a record deal and worked very hard at it. Many were praying for her and waiting for that big moment to happen. After much effort and disappointment she began to cry out to God. "Why did You give me this voice?" He simply answered, "Because I thought you would enjoy it."

chapter nine
the praise life of jesus

One day I thought if I really want to know how to praise the Lord I should look at the lives of some of the great praise leaders in history. After researching a few I realized I was leaving out the most important one: Jesus. I found out some wonderful things about the Savior. If you look deeper in the Scriptures, it is clear what He was like concerning thanksgiving and praise of the Father.

> **And the seventy returned again with joy, saying, Lord, even the devils are subject unto us through thy name.**
>
> **And he said unto them, I beheld Satan as lightning fall from heaven.**
>
> **Behold, I give unto you power to tread on serpents and scorpions, and over all the power of the enemy: and nothing shall by any means hurt you.**
>
> **Notwithstanding in this rejoice not, that the spirits are subject unto you; but rather rejoice, because your names are written in heaven.**
>
> **In that hour Jesus rejoiced in spirit, and said, I thank thee, O Father, Lord of heaven and earth, that thou hast hid these things from the wise and prudent, and hast revealed them unto babes: even so, Father for so it seemed good in thy sight (Luke 10:17-21 KJV).**

This verse was written to describe what happened after seventy disciples came back from a time ministering. On their return they felt bold enough to say, **"Lord, even the devils are subject unto us through thy name" (Luke 10:17 KJV).** I believe I could find a reason to rejoice too if I had seen what they just saw. The truth is I should be seeing that every day, but that is another topic. Verse 21 says in that hour Jesus rejoiced. The first time I read this I passed right over the word "rejoiced" just as if I understood what it really meant. Then one day, while studying the Greek definitions for rejoice, I found the real meaning of what Jesus was doing in the Spirit.

The Greek word, "agalliao" was used when referring to the way that Jesus rejoiced in the Spirit. Agalliao means: "to leap, exult, leap for joy, to show one's joy by leaping and skipping, denoting excessive or ecstatic joy and delight."

Imagine for a moment this scene. The disciples have come back from ministering and seeing miraculous things, and in their excitement they tell Jesus of their adventures. It's probably near dark and they are gathered around a fire where they intend to spend the night. Then without warning, the Master, the Teacher, the center of man's desire, begins to dance. He starts to leap and skip and whirl about with joy. No music, no drums playing, just zeal for God. Did the disciples just stare at Him, astonished by what they saw, or did they join in the celebration? Though there are no further Scriptures describing this scene, I believe hands began to clap, eyes lit up with laughter, and shouts were quick to follow. In a moment seventy men were dancing unashamed before God.

Painting a picture of the Lamb of God acting like a child, as He's whirling about, might have an adverse affect on some. I assure you my goal is to shed some light on the idea of rejoicing before the Lord with all our might, as David did, as Jesus did, and as God Himself does over His people.

JESUS IMITATES HIS FATHER

Then answered Jesus and said unto them, Verily, verily, I say unto you, The Son can do nothing of him-

self, but what he seeth the Father do: for what things soever he doeth, these also doeth the Son likewise.

For the Father loveth the Son, and showeth him all things that himself doeth: and he will show him greater works than these that ye may marvel (John 5: 19-20 KJV).

When Jesus was leaping about rejoicing, He was only doing what He saw His Father doing. We are to marvel, or be stunned as the Greek defines marvel, by what Jesus was seen doing. Jesus did incredible miracles while He walked the earth, but nothing would be more wonderful to watch than the Savior leaping about, enjoying the Father enjoying Him.

God uses the prophet Zephaniah to express Himself concerning His people. His expression is much like Jesus in Luke 10:21.

The LORD thy God in the midst of thee is mighty; he will save, he will rejoice over thee with joy; he will rest in his love, he will joy over thee with singing (Zephaniah 3:17 KJV).

The Hebrew word for **"rejoice"** used here is "suws." It means: "to be bright; cheerful; be glad greatly; make mirth; to enjoy someone." However, when the word **"joy"** is used the second time, it is the Hebrew word "giyl." This means: *"to spin around under the influence of a violent emotion."* The Creator of the universe is cheerful and able to enjoy Himself concerning His people. He is also able to spin around and have violent emotion about us. If God's wrath were big, why wouldn't His joy be big, too?

I believe the prophetic word in Zephaniah 3:17 is acted out in Luke 10:21. Jesus in the midst of His people will save and rejoice over them, while *resting* in His love, and singing over us. As Jesus imitates His Father, we are to imitate Him. Exuberant joy is a part of our heritage.

Zephaniah 3:17 also tells us of God singing. The Hebrew word "rinnah" is used for singing. It means: "creaking, shout of joy, to emit a stridulous sound, gladness, proclamation, singing, triumph." In Psalm 67:4, the psalmist says, **"Let the** nations be glad and sing for joy." "**Nations**" means the rest of the world outside of Israel. "**Sing**" in Psalm 67 is the same Hebrew word used in Zephaniah 3:17, "ranan" or "rinnah". This means we are to shine forth and make a stridulous sound of joy (a joyful noise).

I know it would be hard to imagine just what God would sound like singing, but this gives us some insight on what that might be like. His singing is full of joy and shouts of triumph. If He can speak daylight into being, imagine what His shout of joy is like.

REASONS TO REJOICE

In Luke 10:18 it says that Jesus was watching Satan fall from heaven like lightning. Jesus didn't rejoice over that sight, nor did He rejoice when He gave the disciples power over serpents and all the power of the enemy. He rejoiced over the fact His Father withheld this wisdom from the prudent and gave it to babes (see Luke 10:21).

Just a side note here. In Luke 10:19 Jesus says, **"Behold, I give unto you power to tread on serpents and scorpions, and over all the power of the enemy: and nothing shall by any means hurt you"(KJV).** The word used for **"power"** the first time Jesus speaks is the power He has given His disciples. This word is exousia, and it means: "authority, permission, jurisdiction, liberty superhuman, the power of choke."

"Serpents" means: "cunning and wisdom of man." **"Scorpions"** means: "the sting of death." The second time **"power"** is used it refers to the power of the enemy. This power is the Greek word "dunamis." This means: "power for performing miracles with ability and abundance."

The power Jesus gives a disciple is a greater power than that of the devil. Though the enemy can walk in miracle power, a disciple can walk in permission to use the power of God. He can use his jurisdiction to stop the wisdom of men and stand against the sting of death. He will also not be harmed for doing it. Remember, this power is given to a disciple of Jesus, not just anyone who decides he wants to boss the devil around. This is why He said: make disciples of the nations (see Matthew 28:19). This is also a reason to rejoice in the Lord.

JESUS WAS PRAISED BEFORE HE WAS BORN

> **And it came to pass, that, when Elisabeth heard the salutation of Mary, the babe leaped in her womb; and Elisabeth was filled with the Holy Ghost (Luke 1:41 KJV).**

John the Baptist was leaping for joy while still in the womb of Elisabeth. As a result, she got filled with the Holy Spirit. If we're not afraid to show the joy that comes from our meeting Jesus, others will get saved and filled with the Holy Spirit as a result of that joy (see Psalm 40:3). There is a greater power than we know in the pure joy of knowing the Lord.

> **And Mary said, "My soul doth magnify the Lord,**
> **and my spirit hath rejoiced in God my Saviour" (Luke 1:46-47 KJV).**

Mary is thought to have sung these words to the Lord. The word **"rejoiced"** is the same word used when referring to Jesus praising God in Luke 10:21. Agalliao means to leap about. Mary's spirit was leaping about for joy as she was walking out the will of God.

> **When they saw the star, they rejoiced with exceeding great joy.**
> **And when they were come into the house, they saw the young child with Mary his mother, and fell down, and worshiped him: and when they had opened their treasures, they presented unto him gifts; gold, and frankincense, and myrrh (Matthew 2:10-11 KJV).**

Like King David, these kings rejoiced with exceeding great joy when they beheld the Deliverer. In their culture, falling down, or bowing down, was an act of profound reverence. They were prophetically acting out what the rest of the kings of the world would do one day (see Psalm 86:9 and 110:1). Great rejoicing and worship will always precede Jesus.

> **And suddenly there was with the angel a multitude of the heavenly host praising God, and saying,**
>
> **Glory to God in the highest, and on earth peace, good will toward men (Luke 2:13-14 KJV).**

The praise of Jesus started with Elisabeth and Mary before He was born. Then kings bowed before Him and worshiped a newborn. And suddenly a multitude of the heavenly host came boasting of the glory of God on high. There has always been lots of excitement around Jesus. I believe His presence demands it.

SEEKING THE PRAISES OF MAN

One thing that we can be sure of concerning the life of Jesus on earth; He never sought the praises of man. He never thought it was important to gain the approval of the people to fulfill His destiny. That's not always so with us. We struggle to gain the acceptance of others and consider their reaction as a gauge of our success.

> **For they loved the praise of men more than the praise of God (John 12:43 KJV).**

John uses the Greek word "doxa" for the word "praise." In the classical Greek doza means: "opinion, judgment, conjecture, expectation." When referring to the chief rulers that secretly believed in Jesus, John wrote, they have loved man's approval, opinion, or expectation of them more than God's, so they continued to hide their faith.

These chief rulers, who had power and authority, were afraid of being put out of the synagogue. Somehow the praise and good opinion of the Pharisees was more important to them than the approval of God.

This might serve as a warning to all of us. The Pharisees didn't start out their service to God being **"a brood of vipers,"** as Jesus called them (see Matthew 3:7 NIV). They had good intentions just like we do.

> NOTE: It was interesting to me to find the Pharisees were basically self-appointed. There is no history of where they came from or what tribe of Israel fathered

them. Reference is made to them as far back as 160-140 B.C. They came into power about 76 B.C. and changed the idea of Judaism being a religion into a Law. The interpretation of the Law was their study. They were the developers of a two-fold Law—written and oral. They believed the way to God was through the Law. They opposed Jesus because He refused the teachings of the oral Law.

Sometimes the greatest carriers of the religious spirit are self-appointed people: those trying to meet a need, or fulfill a dream to minister to others. The Pharisees knew that Israel needed God, and they determined by themselves the way for that to happen. Trying to fulfill the needs of the church by human effort is still happening. No matter how you cut this, it is the religious spirit. Praise leaders and musicians can often carry this burden never knowing the worry is meant for intercession. God alone meets the needs of His people. He will use people to meet needs, but He must initiate it.

GOD IS PERFECTING PRAISE

And said unto him, Hearest thou what these say? And Jesus saith unto them, Yea; have ye never read, Out of the mouth of babes and sucklings thou hast perfected praise? (Matthew 21:16 KJV)

I think it's interesting that the Lord used the word **"babes"** when referring to the praises He was perfecting. A "babe" is a child not yet able to speak plainly. And then the word **"perfected"** which means to put a thing in its appropriate position, mature, and complete.

Paraphrasing Matthew 21:16, it could read, "True praise can only be put in its proper place and matured by God, through the mouth of those with child-like trust." If I try to perfect my own praise, I take God out of that task.

PRAISE IS STRENGTH

While on these Scriptures, it's interesting to compare the difference between Psalm 8:2 and Matthew 21:16. Jesus translated the meaning of Psalm 8 in Matthew 21.

> **Out of the mouth of babes and sucklings hast thou ordained strength because of thine enemies, that thou mightest still the enemy and the avenger (Psalm 8:2 KJV).**
>
> **And Jesus saith unto them, Yea; have ye never read, Out of the mouth of babes and sucklings thou hast perfected praise? (Matthew 21:16 KJV)**

Jesus is interpreting Psalm 8 for us. PRAISE is STRENGTH. Ordained strength is full grown praise. This is the praise that stills the enemies of God. Praise is the weapon to still the voice of torment coming against us. The accuser cannot stand while a voice is shouting the praises of God.

Though there are not many Scriptures describing Jesus praising the Father, Luke 10 sure gives us insight on what His feelings were like concerning praise. All those times He went off alone to pray most certainly had to have had some worship time in it.

What happens in private with the Lord is still the most important worshiping life we will ever have. What happened with Jesus in His private time was manifested in His outburst of joy for His Father.

Spontaneous Expression

> **And a very great multitude spread their garments in the way; others cut down branches from the trees, and strewed them in the way.**
>
> **And the multitudes that went before, and that followed, cried, saying, Hosanna to the son of David: Blessed is he that cometh in the name of the Lord; Hosanna in the highest (Matthew 21:8-9 KJV).**

This was the most famous praise and worship session in history. Jesus was making His triumphal entry into Jerusalem, and the people were starting to gather together. When they shouted "Hosanna", they were actually saying, "save, we pray." The root of this word in the Hebrew means a cry for help. Hosanna was somehow changed and used later as a word for praise, but that day the people were crying out for their Deliverer.

This cry was taken from Psalm 118 that was read at the Feast of Tabernacles. Hosanna was shouted on the last day of the Feast. This made it even more offensive to the Pharisees, as this kind of worship was reserved for God at the Holy Feasts.

Though this was a traditional type of response, it was not a traditional reason to have a shouting session in the streets. The people spontaneously began to praise at the coming of Jesus, whether they truly understood what was happening or not. They did a traditional thing in a spontaneous way.

While the Pharisees were wondering what all the noise was about, Jesus was receiving the praise due Him. I don't know if the people of Jerusalem really knew the significance of what they were doing or not. Do we really know the significance of what is happening during praise in church? There are things taking place in the Spirit that our logical mind cannot understand. We are faced with a choice every time we assemble to praise God. Will we be the people in the streets shouting, "Save, we pray," or Pharisees rejecting what they don't want to understand?

EMOTIONALISM

And when the chief priests and scribes saw the wonderful things that he did, and the children crying in the temple, and saying, Hosanna to the son of David; they were sore displeased (Matthew 21:15 KJV).

In Matthew 21:8 the multitude spread their garments on the road and shouted praise. They were outside the city. In verse 15 it says the children were *inside* the temple *crying* and saying Hosanna.

Whenever I see a child crying, or crying out loud as it is defined in the *Lexicon*, I always want to see what the problem is. I assume that crying means there is a problem. When the Pharisees saw the children crying and the people giving the praise to Jesus that was only done at the Feast of Jehovah, they were not only jealous of the response, but they were put off by what they considered to be the over-emotional reaction of everyone that had now manifested itself in these little children crying. They never saw that this was a real response, an act of holy praise to the Savior.

How many times have you thought that some people were getting too emotional for your taste while in a public praise session? I know I have. Yet if God is perfecting praise in the mouths of babes, then we will have to expect emotionalism at times, crying at times, laughing, dancing, and maybe other forms that are spoken of by David in the Psalms such as trembling which means violent shaking (see Psalm 2:11).

All that happens in the presence of the Lord is a reaction or response to that presence. The devil wanted Jesus to fall down and worship as a response to him. His desire was to get the response that was due God alone. Response to someone, like respect, reverence, or bowing can be an act of worship in itself. Since respect and reverencing someone due respect is scriptural, there must be a distinction between my response to my boss or pastor and the presence of God the Almighty.

QUOTES

The following are two quotes from men that have a similar view of what a song of praise and the prophetic have in common.

> *"It is not likely, therefore that Paul would speak of 'psalms inspired by the Spirit...' if he intended the reference to be to the borrowing of traditional odes from the hymn-book of the Jewish Psalter. Compositions which were spontaneously 'inspired' and created for the occasion were much more probably in view."* (Ralph Martin)

> *"Hymn-singing was developed in the first century church by the sect of the Therapeutae. Describing their meetings as one of the group stands up and sings a hymn to God, either a new one which he has composed himself, or an old one by an earlier composer. The others followed one by one in fitting order. In the evening meetings the men and women were separated at first; and would sing hymns, sometimes antiphonally, often accompanying the anthems with rhythmical movements. Then divinely inspired, the men and women together, having become one choir' sing 'hymns of thanks to the Savior God.'"* (Philo)

chapter ten
worship leader/ transparent person

In this chapter I would like to focus on what the church calls "worship leader." There are no Scriptures giving clear instructions on what a worship leader should do, nor are there any Scriptures that even use the words "worship leader," but this job still exists.

I tell this short story to say that if you believe you are a praise leader and the call of the Lord is on you, then get ready to have your heart exposed before all and in the bargain the Lord will make you transparent. Remember, God doesn't need a door to heaven but a window without glass.

After leading praise one Sunday and the presence of the Lord was still strong in the room, a friend came to me with a word he believed was from God. This red-haired prophet smiled and said to me, "The Lord wants to ask you something today. 'Will you go before Me and prepare the hearts of My people for My love, joy, salvation, repentance, mercy, and wrath? Answer before the sun goes down today.'" Of course I answered with a hardy and religious "yes." I had no idea what God would do to me after that and how many ways I would fail to do what He requested.

At first I enjoyed seeing the hearts of God's people open up and receive His love. It was great fun watching many get free as they soaked in His joy. Then there were the times when I knew salvation was on His heart and all would have to wait for that to be completed. I had a harder time with the repentance thing. I usually had to play songs about my own sin as the Spirit convicted others. His mercy always made me weep, which I never liked to do publicly, and finally I knew there had to be warnings about God's wrath.

After some time I realized the way God wanted me to prepare the hearts of His people was to have my own heart exposed. He wasn't interested in me telling the people how to repent, but for me to repent in front of them during praise times. This job of preparing the hearts was much harder than I first thought. He has stopped me in the middle of a song and said, "Someone needs to get saved here, no more singing until they come forward." Much to my surprise, the person in question did come forward and get saved. He has caused me to stop playing during an exciting time of praise because I was trying to make something happen.

There are many other stories about how the Lord interrupted our good times, but He was doing one thing consistently: making me transparent. I would love to say right here, "I'm completely transparent now God, You can stop exposing me," but I know He won't. I also know I'm not completely transparent yet.

I have run away from this call a few times, but I always have to come back. The enemy has also tried to get me to stop by using the lust for success in the world. When I got into ministry and the church system, he stirred up jealousy, fear, and usury against me. The religious spirit has taken his turn by tormenting, and finally discouragement and depression have done more damage than any of other things combined. Still the Lord's love and mercy have called me back again and again to one place. It is impossible for me to stop praising the King who saved me.

MEETINGS WITH GOD

A part of the job of praise leading is drawing near to God and being able to encourage others to do the same. In Genesis 3:8, God is looking for Adam in the Garden. Adam has sinned by eating of The Tree of the Knowledge of Good and Evil, and God is now close and wants to have fellowship with His creation.

Because of sin, Adam's first response to God's presence was to hide. When God said, "Where are you?", He wasn't asking because He didn't know. God was saying, (I'm paraphrasing) "Look where you are."

Anytime we try to draw close to God, we will be faced with the reality of where we are spiritually. Many would rather hide than face this.

A praise leader will be faced with some people who do not really want a meeting with God. They will sometimes reject an opportunity to draw near because of unconfessed sin, or just stay on the surface of praise. The leader will also be faced with those who are willing to make a sacrifice of praise, but cannot find a reason to be cheerful about it.

As a leader, you cannot let the devil control you with these kinds of distractions. Worrying will steal your joy and then the sacrifice will not be accepted. That's just what the enemy wants.

Do not enter into debates with those that question the expression of joy on other worshipers. That is the same religious spirit that demanded the praise to stop when Jesus entered Jerusalem.

THE FIRST WORSHIP LEADER

The first person to try and lead God's people into worship was Moses. He led Israel to Mt. Sinai where they were going to meet their one true God. There was no predicting the outcome of that first attempt at a public worship session. There is no predicting what will happen on Sunday morning when a praise leader tries to lead the Christian church either.

Exodus 19 was the first close encounter the children of Israel had with their God. There were those who had a relationship with the Lord before then, but Moses was the first worship leader to try and join the people together with their Master.

Starting with verse 3 of chapter 19, God talks with Moses when he went up on the mountain. He begins with a reminder that He brought them out of bondage and took care of them. Then He makes this statement:

> 'Now then, if you will indeed obey My voice and keep My covenant, then you shall be My own possession among all the peoples, for all the earth is Mine;
>
> and you shall be to Me a kingdom of priests and a holy nation.' These are the words that you shall speak to the sons of Israel" (Exodus 19:5-6).

Priests were from the family of Aaron, a Levite. They were allowed to draw near to God; however, God's desire is for an entire nation to be called priests and draw near to Him. That remains His desire, and through the blood of Jesus that is now possible.

There are no conditions on God's love, but there are conditions on drawing near to Him. It has always been God's intention that we all are able to draw near to our Master, and not stand at a distance and have only selected people come near to Him. Nevertheless, when the people were faced with the awesomeness of the Almighty, there was quite a reaction.

> **And it came to pass on the third day in the morning, that there were thunders and lightnings, and a thick cloud upon the mount, and the voice of the trumpet exceeding loud; so that all the people that was in the camp trembled (Exodus 19:16 KJV).**

If this entire event happened today, there is no knowing what our reaction would be. Most likely we would do the same thing the Jews did—run. The idea of a close encounter with God is too much for most people to endure.

> **And all the people perceived the thunder and the lightning flashes and the sound of the trumpet and the mountain smoking; and when the people saw it, they trembled and stood at a distance.**
>
> **Then they said to Moses, "Speak to us yourself and we will listen; but let not God speak to us, lest we die."**
>
> **And Moses said to the people, "Do not be afraid; for God has come in order to test you, and in order**

that the fear of Him may remain with you, so that you may not sin."

So the people stood at a distance, while Moses approached the thick cloud where God was (Exodus 20:18-21).

When leading praise in a church, there will always be those that stand far off. Fear of the Lord is the beginning of wisdom, but that fear should cause us to want to come near and not run. The main purpose for the fear of the Lord as stated in verse 20 is to keep us from sin. Those that stand far off from the Spirit are sometimes just watching to see if they really want to enter in, or they may just be judging what is happening. It is also possible they are having a great time in the Spirit, but make no outward gesture at all.

The word **"test,"** in Exodus 19:20, means, "testing the quality of someone through a demonstration of stress." It's under that stress that our true character comes out. This is why praise times can have a tendency to get intense at times. We are being tested more ways than one in that intensity.

THE DONKEY THE LORD RIDES

There is something the Lord revealed to me that may be insulting to some and encouraging to others. I got a word one day from a friend and it was "You are the ass the Lord rides on." After feeling a bit slighted, I began to see the wisdom of this. Then a revelation started to come. I will try to explain.

A praise leader is like the donkey that Jesus rode into Jerusalem on (see Matthew 21:7). Known as a beast of burden, under the yoke, the donkey's job was to carry the burden of His presence, parading the Master down the street for all to see and cheer. The agenda of the animal was not even considered, but only the will of the Lord. He controlled this burden barrier without bit and bridle—the way He said He always wanted to (see Psalm 32:9). He did it by revealing His will to the animal and there was obedience.

The same should happen with a praise leader. Wherever the Lord wants to go should never be contested. The goal was to make it to the other side of Jerusalem.

The donkey hears the same shouts of praise as the rider does, but doesn't feel it's for him. The animal feels the same excitement as his burden does, but doesn't think he is creating it. The donkey gets the honor of walking on the many cloaks of praise that line the street, just because of Who he is carrying.

A donkey is not large enough to carry more than one person. Jesus is not interested in riding double. The animal was selected by the Lord personally. No other person was expected to ride this burden bearer except Jesus. No one would consider asking the Lord to step down so they could take a ride, and no one should challenge Him for the right.

I hope you like my allegory and that you realize the message in it. As I mentioned in the chapter called "Anointing," the song has become the burden barrier of the church now. There must be greater attention paid to who is taking a ride on the donkey, remembering, **"For My yoke is easy My burden is light" (Matthew 11:30, NKJV).**

CHRISTIAN GATHERINGS

Every time Christians come together to enter into worship, the leader is faced with a similar scenario as Moses. The more intense the presence of the Spirit of God gets, the more afraid the people will get. If they reject the intensity, as did the Jews, the only thing left is to make laws to follow, concluding the Spirit is too intense to follow personally. When passion seems to be getting out of human control, then the spirit of religion jumps up and takes over. Backing off is generally the result.

Personal notes:

1. I've been in some pretty wild praise times with a large group of people. As long as I didn't focus on the wildness, but on the Lord, it never got out of control, even when it seemed there was no stopping it. A few seconds of playing a gentile song to the

Lord brought it back down without complaint. The fact is: I've never been in an "out-of-control" praise time. Since we don't have any Scriptures telling us to limit our zeal for God, or to beware of those showing too much joy and exuberance when praising, then chances are we won't ever really be out of control.

2. There are times when the enemy sends distractions into the praise time. His hope is to gain attention. Giving even more attention to God and intercession usually stops that. God chooses to reveal Himself in many different ways. It would be foolish to think He only does things one way. A burning bush that wasn't consumed got the attention of Moses. Mt. Sinai trembling and thunder in the sky with smoke covering the mountain is how He decided to reveal Himself to Israel. Elijah heard God in the midst of the storm as a wee small voice. You must be careful, as a praise leader, to not assume God will only move one way, or speak to His people one way. If you try to predict how God will move among His people, you will surely miss Him.

HOW CAN THE MUSICIANS STAND?

Taking another look at Exodus 20:18, you'll find the people were all afraid to come close to God, yet the trumpets kept blowing during the thunder and all that intense activity. Why weren't the trumpet players afraid too?

I believe the answer is that God will gird up the musicians for the work that must be done. They will have an uncommon strength to sustain long worship times and draw near to His presence without fainting. The music that the Spirit is releasing in this time will draw people to the mountain of the Lord. It will be each man's own decision if he chooses to run or not.

> **"Behold, I am going to send My messenger, and he will clear the way before Me. And the Lord, whom you seek, will suddenly come to His temple;**

and the messenger of the covenant, in whom you delight, behold, He is coming," says the LORD of hosts.

"But who can endure the day of His coming? And who can stand when He appears? For He is like a refiner's fire and like fullers' soap.

"And He will sit as a smelter and purifier of silver, and He will purify the sons of Levi and refine them like gold and silver, so that they may present to the LORD offerings in righteousness" (Malachi 3:1-3).

As you can see, there will be a cleansing of the motives of the praise leaders. The Lord will come as a refiner's fire and consume all that is not of Him.

JUDGMENT IN THE HOUSE OF THE LORD

We all know that judgment comes to the house of the Lord first (see I Peter 4:17), but what I failed to see in these Malachi Scriptures is, He is coming to the Levites before He comes to the church. All the false motives of the praise leaders and musicians will be tried before He judges the church. Looking at verse 4 and 5 show God's intent.

"Then the offering of Judah and Jerusalem will be pleasing to the LORD, as in the days of old and as in former years.

"Then I will draw near to you for judgment: and I will be a swift witness against the sorcerers and against the adulterers and against those who swear falsely, and against those who oppress the wage earner in his wages, the widow and the orphan, and those who turn aside the alien, and do not fear Me," says the LORD of hosts (Malachi 3:4-5).

I know it is difficult to be under God's refining fire while the rest of the church is silently asking, "what's wrong with you?" If some of that has already happened to you as a leader, don't worry, it will happen again.

One time while I was leading, and about two thousand people were jumping up and down, I heard the Spirit say, "This is NOT God." I kept looking at the people having a great time and starting to rebuke that spirit of condemnation. Still I heard, "This is NOT God." Finally I had to stop, and confess to the people that I had been trying to make something happen and I was guilty of not waiting for the Spirit's leading before we started.

I could feel an expectancy from the people and the leadership to repeat a powerful move of the Spirit we had on another occasion. Whether that expectancy was real or imagined, it was there nonetheless. I was doing my best to fulfill all the hopes that were building up in that room. The only problem was, "This is NOT God."

We all know that a praise leader is not the presence of the Lord, only a vessel, but our hearts rely on what we have seen a man do and not what we have seen God do. I knew I was in this situation and all that was left to do was stop.

I repented as did many of the people, and there was a time of real seeking of the Lord for the band members and me. I couldn't tell if the leadership was in agreement with me or not as I was too afraid to look in their direction. After about fifteen minutes of prayer and repentance, this interrupted meeting started to have the Spirit of the Lord in it. There was a slow rise of joy starting to happen, and the band and I broke into a spontaneous song that lasted about thirty minutes. It was the only truly anointed time of praise we had at this three-day conference.

I was personally having a battle with the requests of men and the man-pleasing spirit that I struggle with constantly. At the end of this time I asked the Lord how to get through things like this in the future. He gave me an impression that I must turn the expectancy of man into faith by first making proclamations of faith in song, then by pointing all attention and admiration toward Him. The Holy Spirit is here to guide us into that kind of proclamation and directed admiration, but I must be listening to do that.

INTENSE

Praise is going to get more and more intense. That intensity is the predecessor to God's actual presence. The scene on Mt. Sinai was only an example of what the intensity of God is like. Instead of backing off and preferring a relationship with God through Moses, they should have fallen down and worshiped their Deliverer. Will we stand far off, or come closer and let God prove us through a demonstration of stress? There is no telling what the outcome of our next real encounters with God will be like.

Let me add a little balance to this. When I speak of intensity, I'm not only referring to screaming and wild dancing and throwing yourself around (as if under the influence of a violent emotion), but of an intensity of God's presence. Sometimes the reaction to Him will be weeping or falling on your face before His glory. Other times it is hands raised in complete adoration of the Master. Then there is the broken and contrite man who can only bow low before his King. Praising God and reacting to Him must be a spontaneous act from the heart. God *is* intense; we're not. Beware, as a praise leader, to not coerce others into acting intense when praising. If their reaction to an intense time with God is intense, so be it.

A WINDOW TO HEAVEN

I don't believe that God is looking for a praise leader to be a door to the heavens. I think He wants windows without glass to serve in His house. Being transparent before God and man is the first step in becoming a window without glass. Let me show you what I have seen so far concerning this. Aside from the fact that leading praise can prove to be a spiritually dangerous job in the church, there are fundamental things that should be considered before taking this position.

In II Chronicles 20:19, Jehoshaphat (king of Judah) had sought the Lord for a victory over the enemies that surrounded Judah (see chapter 3 of this book, "Praise as a Strategy"). After the divine answer came, Jehoshaphat bowed low to the ground.

The people of Judah did as their king did and bowed low, too. Then a group of Levites from the children of Korah and Kohath stood up and began to lead by giving a praise response to the Lord in a loud voice. They were leading praise that had faith in it. Perhaps they saw the angels in heaven shouting and praising God so they just responded to that, or maybe they just had an impression that God needed to be praised in a more jubilant way. In whatever way they determined to do this in the midst of people on their faces, I don't know, but they became windows to heaven right then, and all of Judah followed their lead. That's what it means to be transparent before God.

WORSHIP IN FAITH

It is my belief that the Lord is showing us how to worship in faith as well as Spirit and Truth. Jesus said in Matthew 17:20, **"If you SAY to this mountain, be. . . cast into the sea. . ."** (NKJV). We must say with our mouths. There are things we must proclaim out loud, even when we don't see any victory yet. The walls of Jericho were torn down by the power of God, but not until the shout of victory went up. It was a shout in faith.

God spoke to Joshua and said, **"See, I have given into thy hand Jericho, and the king thereof, and the mighty men of valor"** (Joshua 6:2 ASV). God was commanding Joshua to SEE in faith that the city would fall into his hands. He had given him the victory over the city, even when the walls were still standing. Joshua had only to walk it out.

Though marching around Jericho was a strange event, the people were accustomed to following the priests carrying the Ark. The Levites used the faith the people had in them to fulfill the purposes of Joshua who was fulfilling the purposes of God. They worshiped (served) in faith.

We've all seen people following a musical trend or a band they like a lot. They will follow praise, when it is anointed, the same way. A time is coming when anointed praise will be listened to more than any other kind of music. The truth will be all anyone wants to hear and faith will come by hearing.

COMMITMENT IN SONG

Singing the Word of God and singing the truths that are promised us are no different than saying them (see Romans 10:17). We are no less obligated to fulfill our commitments to God because we sang them in a song on Sunday, than we are after a tearful commitment. When you lead songs like "I Surrender All," you must know that God is now expecting a complete surrender to Him. Our praise will become a dreadful noise to Him if we do not honor what we've committed to Him.

I believe the days are over when we come together and make strong statements of faith in a song and do not walk it out. Faith without works is dead, even when you just sing it (see James 2:26). If you are a praise leader, be sure of what you are singing and causing others to sing with you, because God hears you and takes you at your word.

LEARNING TO WAIT ON THE LORD

Waiting on God was the hardest thing I've ever done. I had learned a long time ago, "You gotta keep the show rolling," so to get to a place of waiting proved to be quite a challenge. In most cases, I was too worried about the service going well to wait for the Holy Spirit to do something.

God's patience with me has been without measure, as I blundered into places in the Spirit I had no business going. When I should have waited, I moved forward. When I should have taken a more aggressive step, I delayed. Both are very dangerous.

Slowly, with the encouragement of a pastor, I found some ways to wait for the Spirit to give me instructions.

As the praise leader, no matter how much you may feel you are hearing God about change in the way your church is moving in worship, nothing will change until the leadership is in wholehearted agreement with you. God will not honor , what you are doing without the leadership being respected and in place.

The Holy Spirit began to convince me to stop making a song list on Saturday night. He would say, "Just let Me lead you." Though we all talk about how wonderful it is to be led by the Spirit, we really don't often completely let Him do that.

Sunday was fearful at first, but later became great fun. I always seem to do better when under pressure and no real understanding of where I'm going. However, I started a lot of trouble in the church when it sounded like I was lost. The band was embarrassed when I would go off in the Spirit and they didn't know where that was. Yes, following the Holy Spirit is not a pretty thing at first. There were many times when self-consciousness overcame me and the desire to please got very strong. The people would reward me with approval when I'd return to the traditions they were accustomed to. They would also rejoice like they never had before when I found what the Spirit wanted.

The best way to learn to follow the Spirit in worship is to do it as much as possible at home or in a small, trusted group. Waiting is less painful and there are fewer distractions. There's something about Sunday morning that really brings out that religious spirit that says, "I just want church to go well and not too long." A musician wandering around in the Spirit, trying to find what to do next, will bring some real strain into church.

That's why it's best to practice this at home. Sometimes you may find that your real calling to leading praise is at home and not at church at all.

WAITING HAS MANY FORMS

One way to wait on God is to play a praise song and keep going until something begins to break in the resistance to the Spirit. Or just play instrumentally for a time and stay in a posture of praise. The Hebrew word "zamar" means: "to play the strings of the instrument in celebration." David did that for Saul and the tormenting spirits left him (see I Samuel 16:16).

Make sure the instrumentalists are skilled as this was the requirement in Scripture. Do not "doodle" on the instrument;

that means just playing around or experimenting on the instrument without real purpose. This is not an opportunity to show off either, though that is always in question when a musician starts playing instrumentally. Make what you are playing an extension of what you were just singing. That doesn't just mean the melody, but the emotion of the singing. The instrumental portion of the song is supposed to cause people to reflect or begin to sing their own song to the Lord. If the band is just trying to impress the crowd, there will be no pondering the Lord. They will soon get sick of the instrumental parts, and start making excuses for why they don't think you should try those kinds of things. Don't give up trying right away if it takes longer than you thought to find the Spirit. He sometimes plays hard-to-get in order to strengthen your resolve to find Him.

Talk to a long distance runner sometime. He will tell you that there is something that happens in you when you have gone a long way. There is a feeling that can only be experienced by running that distance. The same is true in the Spirit. There is something that happens after you have prayed or praised a long time. Intercessors understand this idea.

(There is more about waiting on the Lord in the last chapter called "The Practical Side of Praise.")

MEANING OF LEADER

The word "leader" means "guide" in the New Testament. In the Hebrew it means: "commander as occupying the front, military or religious, captain, chief etc." Another word in the Greek that means leader is "epairo" which means "to raise up." Worship leader literally translates: "military or religious guide to the bowing low and serving of God." If you feel qualified to guide others into serving the Lord, then calling yourself a "worship leader" is OK.

I'd rather say that a worship leader in church should be called a "praise leader" because praise is the weapon we use to get to the place of worship. Once we get in God's presence we all know how to "bow low and serve." If you try to lead that worship, you will be getting in the way.

FALLEN PRAISE LEADER

Satan was created to lead the praise in heaven (see Ezekiel 28:13-14). Every time we praise God and lead others into that position, we are displacing the devil, and doing the very thing he was created to do.

Imagine being created for a job, and then leaving that position. Even if you wanted to leave, you may hope that your absence would create a void that couldn't be filled. Satan may have felt that his leaving this awesome job would bring a silence to all praise. Well it didn't. The entire body of Christ is now shouting the praises of God, and anyone leading that praise will be subject to the resentment and jealousy that only Satan can bring.

The human being was designed to worship and praise. The devil would like that praise to be directed at him. Every time we praise and lead others into praising God, we deal another death-blow to the enemy's plan to draw all praise to him. That is another reason why leading praise is an awesome but dangerous job.

RECOGNITION

> **And he led Him up and showed Him all the kingdoms of the world in a moment of time.**
>
> **And the devil said to Him, "I will give You all this domain and its glory; for it has been handed over to me, and I give it to whomever I wish.**
>
> **Therefore if You worship before me, it shall all be Yours."**
>
> **And Jesus answered and said to him, "It is written, 'You shall worship the Lord your God and serve Him only'" (Luke 4:5-8).**

When the devil tried to get Jesus to worship him, the Greek translates **"worship"** with two words. The first is proskuneo: "kiss the hand, as a dog is at his masters hand"; and the second is "enopion", which means "to look at the face or respond to the presence of someone; towards which another turns his eyes."

Satan wanted Jesus to recognize his presence as someone worthy. His goal was to have recognition. Not just recognition from anyone, but real acknowledgment from the Lord Himself.

The devil knew that if he got Jesus to recognize him all others would follow. The battle we are still in is the enemy's efforts to get us to recognize him and not the Lord. The devil is not asking anyone to love him, only to recognize and serve him. Personal recognition was Lucifer's greatest transgression.

It's a musician's need for affirmation that usually causes him to seek recognition, believing that will fix that need. Only God can truly affirm someone to where they won't need endless doses of it to survive. Satan wants a praise leader to seek recognition for himself, while the Spirit wants us to look for God and the affirmation that comes from Christ-likeness.

Desiring recognition can come in a few different forms making it hard to "recognize." Sometimes a leader will use the silent act, hoping all will look their way to find out what they are silent about. Others will fill the stage with all kinds of instruments or things that draw much attention to themselves. Self-importance is an effective tool in being recognized. Then there are the ones who will STOP everything when they're having trouble hearing themselves well enough, or make subtle demands for others to be subordinate to them. They will sometimes privately ask people in the congregation if they can be heard, and if there is any question about their audibility, they will go after the sound man as if he were the devil himself.

My personal way of seeking recognition was to subtly tell everyone all the famous people I worked with over the years. I guess I was trying to make myself credible without having to really play.

I could fill a book on ways musicians use to be recognized, but the most important fact about this is, it is what Satan wanted most of all.

SING YOUR HEART

In a traditional praise service many great hymns are sung, and some of the new songs that are being written for praise are full of joy for the Lord. But at some point in that service it is important for the people to express their own feelings toward God. Since many people are too inhibited to do something like that, they need some encouragement. I have found when I sing my own heart to God, it is almost always the general heart of the people in that gathering. It's a simple concept: When like-minded people come together, they are like-minded. Each one may have a different set of circumstances governing their lives, but for the most part they will be of like-minds concerning Jesus.

I wait for the Spirit to give me direction on how to come before the Throne. Sometimes it's expressing the lovingkindness of God, as that group needs to hear of that part of God's character. Sometimes singing the praises of God with all your might is needed. Then at times it's standing strong in the Spirit and interceding for families who are lost. It's learning how to unite the body for the purposes of God.

King David was able to sing his own heart before the Lord and when his complaints, prophecies, and adorations went up to heaven, God called it all praise. The Hebrew word for the entire book of Psalms is TeHILLAH, which is a technical and musical term for a song that exalts God. All the Psalms express the heart of the writer. Some of them express the heart of all Israel. Some speak of God's lovingkindness for His people; some tell of His wrath. What I'm getting at is Sunday morning should be an expression of your heart to God and His heart for His people. It doesn't always have to be conventional. God is not afraid of or offended by your reality.

Keep a balance if you are leading praise. Be sure not to use the church for your personal complaining center. If you look at the Psalms as your example, you'll find there is almost always some kind of resolve or victory to every trouble. God is that victory and His joy is our strength.

COMMUNICATION BETWEEN GOD AND HIS PEOPLE

Learning to communicate with God and then with His people should be a praise leader's ambition. The reward for that is not the reaction of the people, but what is gained by communing with God.

You can actually be instructed on how to do that, but it must come from skillful people. I Chronicles 15:22 tells us that was a requirement of the Levites. However, no matter how much we read or how much teaching on this subject you get, there is no substitute for time with God. You learn to communicate with the Lord by communing with Him. God is not only about learning and intellectual ascent. He is a God of experience and reality. If you take time with the King, you will find He is touchable and willing to speak to you.

Similarly, you get to know God's people by spending time with them as well. Spending time with people doesn't mean listening to their complaints and writing that into your next praise song, but seeking God's heart for those people. If you quiet yourself on Sunday morning, you will begin to feel what is on the heart of the people coming in the door. Sin actually cries out in the spirit to be stopped (see Genesis 18:20). Disease has its own sound; a need for encouragement is often easy to notice; the desire for more of the Lord is usually just under the surface of most people. With some tuning, a praise leader can find the heart of God and the heart of His people, and that can all happen within a few minutes of the time to start. You must be brave enough to wait and quiet enough to hear.

I know that ten minutes before praise starts, everyone on the praise team is praying their guts out, begging God to come and do something in the service. In spite of all this, the leader must be able to hear the Spirit before any real determination of what to do is discerned. If not, you will be destined to repeat yourself Sunday after Sunday.

chapter eleven
what is an acceptable sacrifice?

Have you ever wondered what God is thinking concerning the way we praise Him? I have thought, at times, that He couldn't possibly enjoy the way we try to come close to Him. Other times I thought He must be blessed with this great shout of joy.

Since there is no applause meter sent down from heaven, the strength of His presence has been our gauge for understanding acceptable praise. Even if there seems to be no presence of the Spirit, we keep right on going with the business of church.

This, of course, is for the sake of the meeting going well. The desire to have a meeting go well has somehow overcome a lot of churches. That desire has even quenched the Spirit at times.

No matter what our agenda might be for a time of praise, there are some rules that God Himself has established pertaining to this sacrifice.

SACRIFICE

Almost all of the Greek and Hebrew words for "sacrifice" say "offering." Some say "kill, gift, or oblation." One of the definitions for offering is "to draw near." A sacrifice or offering can mean to draw near to God; in other words, the cost of drawing near to God.

If you want to get to know someone, there will have to be a sacrifice involved in some way. If I want to go to someone's house to visit, there will be a sacrifice of going. The effort it will take to get out of my private life (comfort zone), and enter into the cost of being a friend to someone, is an offering made to that friendship. In the English language we say we are "going to someone's house." The Hebrew would see that as "drawing near" to someone. Using that idea, we are not "going" to church, but "drawing near" to God, showing our willingness to pay the cost of that relationship.

God wanted this relationship so bad that He made the Supreme sacrifice to get it. There is no question that God understands sacrifice and the true meaning of the offering it takes to draw near to someone. It would stand to reason then, if we want to know more about the "sacrifice of praise," we should go to the Lord for that answer.

THE FIRST OFFERING

> **And in process of time it came to pass, that Cain brought of the fruit of the ground an offering unto the LORD.**
>
> **And Abel, he also brought of the firstlings of his flock and of the fat thereof. And the LORD had respect unto Abel and to his offering:**
>
> **But unto Cain and to his offering he had not respect. And Cain was very wroth, and his countenance fell (Genesis 4:3-5, KJV).**

This is the example that would show us how to pay the cost of drawing near to God. It is interesting to note that Cain made his offering from his excess not his first fruits. The first words at the beginning of verse 3 are, **"And in process of time. . . ."** This means the end. It was at the end of the harvest when all things were accomplished and all the excess was accounted for that Cain made his offering. The time to be grateful to God is not at the end of all things, but at the beginning.

After Cain's offering was not respected and his countenance fell, the Lord gave him instructions on how to make an offering acceptable to Him.

If thou doest well, shalt thou not be accepted? and if thou doest not well, sin lieth at the door. And unto thee shall be his desire, and thou shalt rule over him (Genesis 4:7 KJV).

God does not mention the way that Cain's offering would be acceptable, but how he would be made acceptable. Cain would be accepted if he did well in his offering. This word **"well"** in the Hebrew is "towb." It means to be: *"cheerful, merry, fair, prosperity"*. God is saying the way to make an offering to Him, that the person offering will be accepted, is to do it with a cheerful heart. Make your sacrifice to Him with joy. The word **"accepted"** (Hebrew word seh-ayth') means: *"to be raised up, dignify, exaltation in rank, or character"*.

In summary of this verse, if we want to draw near to God, we will have to make a cheerful offering of our desire to know Him, and in the doing we will be lifted up and our rank and character will be exalted.

A paraphrased version of verse 7 might read; "If you can find joy in My choosing your brother's sacrifice over yours, I will lift you up."

Have you ever been passed over when it came time to be considered for the praise team? Did you feel as though you were being treated unfairly? Did you think you could be doing that job better than the one up there? If the answer is yes to all these questions, then it's time you realized these things happened to you to see if you would embrace joy and acceptance of God's choice for this hour. If we all knew that there was a greater blessing in accepting God's choice with joy, there wouldn't be as much envy, strife, and jealousy in the church.

There is a cost involved in drawing near to God, whether He accepts your sacrifice or not. I know this may not sound like the "nice-guy-God" we are used to, but just singing a song to the Lord does not mean He will accept it as praise. There is only one verse in the Bible that says He inhabits the praises (TeHillah) of Israel (see Psalm 22:3). It is the condition of the heart that causes the Lord to inhabit this sacrifice, just like it has always been (see Psalm 51:16-17).

CAIN KILLED ABEL

In verse 8, it says that Cain talked with Abel and when they got out into the field, Cain killed his brother. What did Cain and Abel talk about? What could have been said that would cause a man to kill his own brother? How did this incident turn into such hate?

I've been corrected by God before, and I never felt anything but love and comfort, even when the correction seemed harsh. I don't believe that Cain's hatred came from his chastisement. Somehow, Abel spoke the right words that put Cain into a rage. Have you ever found yourself feeling angry because of someone else's favor? Sometimes we feel justified in resenting someone with favor if they are not as humble as we think they should be.

There are more questions in these verses than one can imagine, but God makes it clear what happened to Cain in the second half of verse 7. **"If thou doest not well, sin lieth at the door; and unto thee shall be his desire, and thou shalt rule over him" (KJV).**

Cain did not find his joy, and sin was waiting to take advantage of that situation. The only way out is to rule over its influence in your life. Cain needed to master the desire sin had for him. We must do the same.

Here is an interesting note on the names of Cain and Abel. Cain means "possession," and Abel means "breath." Breath is another word for spirit. Being possessive will often kill the Spirit of another.

A RIGHTEOUS SACRIFICE

The sacrifices of praise we make to God will be made righteous by the refining fire of the Lord (see Malachi 3:1-4). Then the offerings of Judah and Jerusalem will be righteous and acceptable to Him. A heart full of joy for the Lord and His choices is a righteous sacrifice.

chapter twelve
dipping your hand in the bowl

And as they were eating, He said, "truly I say to you that one of you will betray Me."

And being deeply grieved, they each one began to say to Him, "Surely not I, Lord?"

And He answered and said, "He who dipped his hand with Me in the bowl is the one who will betray Me" (Matthew 26:21-23).

This Scripture refers to the one man that betrayed Jesus, but it also represents a characteristic that can be found in betrayers, and contains a warning for all of us, especially those called to minister in the body of Christ.

The bowl of oil represents the anointing. The bread that is dipped into it represents the word. We all know that when the word is spoken with anointing, it tastes a lot better. Jesus is the Anointed One. When He takes the bread of life and reaches for the anointing, all others should wait until He has used all the oil He wants.

I don't believe anyone who loves Jesus would ever consciously betray Him, but there are things that happen regularly in meetings that do betray His purposes. Certainly it is good to want to dip our hands in the oil, and it is good to seek the anointing of the Lord, but if we have a tendency to crowd in to use the anointing when Jesus is moving, it reveals a presumption that can lead to our becoming a stumbling block to His purposes.

What Is the Anointing

The oil is a symbol of God's power manifested through the Holy Spirit. As I mentioned above, the oil that was used at the last supper was for dipping bread to soften it and make it more palatable. The other biblical uses of oil were for anointing a person for healing, setting apart (sanctifying), appointment to an office, or embalming. God commanded Moses to anoint the tabernacle of the congregation and its contents (see Exodus 30:25-28). Anything that was to be used in the house of the Lord had to be anointed for the job. "Sanctified" or "set aside" is what anointing really means, and the priests that would minister before the Presence had to be anointed before they could be near the Lord.

The Lord gave very specific instructions about the ingredients used in this oil. As I mentioned earlier in the chapter called "Anointing," the anointing oil was made by a perfumer (see Exodus 30:25), and was used to pour over the heads of those who were to come into the presence of God. One had to be anointed to be a priest and to serve in the Tent of the Lord. Even objects in the Tabernacle had to be anointed to make them sacred. Moses, Aaron, and Aaron's sons had to be anointed to fulfill the call on their lives (see Exodus 28:41). The servants of God will always need to be anointed in order to fulfill their call or walk out a task given by the Lord.

In these examples, the people anointed were chosen for the job. They did not choose themselves to be anointed. As Christians, we often feel that we have only to choose what we want to be in life, and in many cases we can bring that to pass. However, that may not be how God wants us to operate concerning the anointing. We cannot fully know what God's purposes are for us until our hearts have been changed. We must be devoted to Him and not just seeking our own imaginings. The anointing is to be received with thanksgiving, but it is not to be grabbed, which reveals a selfishness or ambition, both of which will lead to a misuse of the anointing.

THE HAND

It is significant that in Matthew 26:23 Jesus said **"He who dipped his hand with Me in the bowl is the one who will betray Me."** They were dipping bread in the oil to soften it, but Jesus said **"hand."** Luke 22:21 also uses **"hand"** when referring to the betrayer. Mark 14:20 refers to the one who dips with Me. The Greek word translated "hand" in these texts is cheir, which means: *"literally or figuratively power; especially [by Hebraism] a means or instrument; hollowness for grasping."* When we see "hand" in this context, it means the instrument of power, or instrument for grasping.

Traditionally, the bowl at the center of the table filled with oil was called a common dish, and anyone that dipped his bread in the dish was to do it in such a way as not to let his finger touch the contents of the dish. If this happened, the oil would be defiled. We, too, can defile the anointing oil if we put our hand into it presumptuously as Judas did. There is a difference between the presence of the Lord and the anointing of the Lord. The anointing is applied to someone to complete a Spirit-led task and is to be done with grace and power. His presence is assured when two or more gather in His name. When we gather in His name, it is usually to honor and praise Him. Judas means "He shall be praised." His name is another name for Judah, which means, "praise." This shows that it is possible to betray the Lord even when our intention is to praise Him. This can happen when we begin to think that because of our praise, we have earned the right to use Him.

SETTING THE TABLE

The job of a praise leader is, metaphorically speaking, to set the table and present to the Lord the sacrifice of true praise that He might accept it. Since Christ is in us, our hope of glory, (see Colossians 1:27) His presence comes up from those who praise Him. His presence will bring life and power to the event we are having, but we must remember that He did not come to our event, nor is His presence an endorsement for the event. He came to inhabit the praises of hungry people (see Psalm 22:3). Jesus is the Anointed One or the anointing at a meeting. We must not grab for the power His presence brings and try to use it to enhance our agenda.

However, when His presence comes many get anxious and presumptuous, and often reach for the oil. It's like a large family at the dinner table, trying to patiently wait for Dad to finish praying before the kids attack the food. It is almost impossible to just leave those powerful times alone.

When I play my guitar and His presence is there, I sound great. When I play the guitar and His presence is not there, I sound average. So I naturally want His presence there so I can always sound great. God's presence doesn't mean I'm an anointed guitar player, but I sure sound like an anointed player when His presence is there. This is what can lead many to grabbing at the anointing. If someone stays on that track, they will most certainly end up betraying the purposes of the Lord.

This is what happened to Judas. He thought he was making an improvement on the purposes of God by betraying His Anointed, and the dipping of his hand into the oil was the act of presumption that made him wish he had never been born (see Matthew 26:24).

Oswald Chambers wrote in his book *My Utmost for His Highest* for January 25, "As workers for God we have to learn to make room for God-to give God 'elbow room.'" He warns against looking for God to come in a particular way, rather than just looking for God. I was surprised that he said we have to learn to make room. This means that we do not do it naturally or automatically.

Taking time to wait on God while in a meeting may seem like too much tension. I know I have tried to say something when the anointing was not present that I thought would be a blessing, but I usually just quenched what was left of the Spirit.

After a few failures, I found that the Lord was willing to let us know who or what He wanted to anoint for that gathering, if we were willing to wait.

Once at a MorningStar conference, the praise was raising up from the people, and there was a sweet spirit in the air. Bob Jones was there and he got up in the middle of praise and said, "There's an anointing for healing here." As soon as he said healing started happening all over the room. His ability to discern the purpose of the anointing in that meeting was a key to making room for the Lord. Many were healed that night. I didn't know what the Lord wanted to do while I was leading praise, but Bob did. It will seldom be the responsibility of only one person to discern all that the Lord wants to do in a single meeting. There wasn't much preaching that night, but there was a lot of healing. This idea really messes with traditional church and many will surely complain about such things, but one day waiting on the Lord will be common in the body.

"WITH ME"

When Jesus said **"he who dipped his hand with Me" (see Matthew 26:35)**, He was making a statement about His relationship with Judas. Meta is the Greek word used for **"with"** in this text, and is defined as *"denoting accompaniment; amid; occupying an intermediate position between, being close to something verses being away."* This word indicates something between being close and being far away. Lukewarm might be another definition. We can be close to Jesus and the things that He does without being intimate with Him. Judas was familiar with Jesus, but John was intimate. There is a difference.

In order to have a covenant meal with the Lord, one must be close with the Lord. The only one that dipped and ran, so to speak, was Judas. We need to examine how we approach the Lord in praise and in other ways in a meeting. Are we just dipping or grasping for the anointing and then leaving to do what we want? Or are we waiting to see what the Lord wants to do?

Jesus was not just breaking bread with His friends to have another meal: He was establishing how all of mankind could enter into the covenant meal while bringing to memory the life and sacrifice of the Messiah. This was the most important meal ever taken. It was certainly not the time to be presumptuous. Those who would behave this way in such a setting are in danger of mishandling the anointing, or even worse, like Judas, betraying it.

This is not to create a paralysis concerning the anointing or power of God, as the Lord uses people to carry out His will all the time. In fact, He has made Himself strangely dependent on His people. However, we must guard against the presumptuous act of continuing on with our own agenda when the Holy Spirit is obviously present and working to do something else. That is the place of sensitivity to which all that minister must come, and it will only come through intimacy with the Lord.

BETRAY

Paradidomi [par-ad-id-o-mee), is Greek for betray and it means: *"to give into the hands (of another) to give over into (one's) power or use; to use, to take care of, to manage."* It really means to control someone else, and in this case, it meant to control the power of Jesus. Many scholars and historians believe Judas betrayed the Lord to compel Him to take His authority as King. Obviously he did not expect the Lord to be crucified because of the great remorse he demonstrated by taking his own life. This probably seemed like a noble thing to Judas at the time, simply forcing the Lord's hand a little bit.

The presumption of thinking that we know better than God Himself will lead to the tragic opposition of His purposes. The Lord has delegated authority to many people, but it is never to be used to control others. If we try to control others with our authority, we will soon try to control the Lord.

If I were to paraphrase Matthew 26:23, it would read something like, "The one who grasps at the power of the anointing at the same time I do, is lukewarm, not close or sensitive to Me, and he will presumptuously use that power to accomplish his own objectives."

GIVING OVER THE POWER

Every time the Holy Spirit activates an anointing on someone, there is a risk of acting presumptuously toward it or using it for our own agenda. Learning to minister with sensitivity to the Lord is going to be the most important issue facing the praise leaders of the next generation. So many musicians, like me have been willing to give away the gifts and power they have for acceptance and approval. If that is the attitude of a praise leader with an anointing on his life, then he will give the power of that anointing away, too.

WARNING

I have been guilty of this time and time again, and know how painful it is to be convicted of this betrayal. It is in fact a betrayal of the purpose of God.

Before the great outpouring of the Spirit promised can happen (see Acts 2:17), there must be some reflection on the way we have already treated the anointing. If we continue to be presumptuous with the anointing, we are in danger of following the same course as Judas.

BINDING THE YOUNG CHAMPIONS

In the story of Samson, the young champion, there were two threats to his godly purpose on earth. One was a woman and the other was praise. This may sound confusing, but let me show you what I mean.

This young champion was agitated and stirred by the Spirit of God to begin to stand under the oppression of the Philistines. **"And the Spirit of the LORD began to stir him** (Samson) **in Mahaneh-dan, between Zorah and Eshtaol" (Judges 13:25).** He was being trained by the Spirit to wake up Israel from the spiritual sleep it was in and fight against the enemies of God. The word **"stir"** in this verse means: *"to* *beat regularly or agitate, or be disturbed"*. The Holy Spirit did all of this.

We, as the church, will sometimes fall into a spiritual sleep and need to be awakened or agitated when necessary. The Spirit of the Lord was creating such a man. There are some young praise leaders who are stirring and even agitating the church, but we must heed the warning that is in these Scriptures.

> **Then the Philistines went up and camped in Judah, and spread out in Lehi.**
>
> **And the men of Judah said, "Why have you come up against us?" And they said, "We have come up to bind Samson in order to do to him as he did to us."**
>
> **Then 3,000 men of Judah went down to the cleft of the rock of Etam and said to Samson, "Do you not know that the Philistines are rulers over us? What then is this that you have done to us?" And he said to them, "As they did to me, so I have done to them."**
>
> **And they said to him, "We have come down to bind you so that we may give you into the hands of the Philistines" (Judges 15:9-12).**

The men of Judah (praise) were the ones used to bind God's champion and give him over to the enemies of the faith. They were betraying God's anointed.

I used to speak to young potential praise leaders with hopes that the traditional church would be more accepting of them.

Some had real wild ideas and others were deeply committed to the Lord. My time with them consisted of trying to slightly cool what was in their hearts. They would say to me, "I just want to shout to the people and say: 'wake up!'" I would smile and remember the slow death my own zeal had. I had learned it was difficult for the whole church to receive a blessing from those kinds of outbursts of passion, and to a pastor just trying to stay alive until next Sunday, those young champions were not what the doctor ordered.

So an older, more compliant praise leader, like me, was used to bind the hands of these young ones. I did this because I carried a man-pleasing spirit and knew what the leadership wanted. No one could be blamed but me for allowing this spirit to bind me. When the Lord began to convict me of this, I wept for those that I may have tied. Now, I am one of those shouting a wake-up call.

If we are too apathetic to recognize the sleep we are being comforted into, then the Lord will raise up young champions who have been stirred by the Spirit. They will start fights with the enemies of God, and the church will be faced with either waking up or binding the hands of these champions.

chapter thirteen
the practical side of praise

I feel it is important to look at some practical aspects of praise in the church. How to get started, how to choose the right people, how big a band, etc? There are a few questions that I've been asked on more than one occasion, so I'll repeat them, and hope they are not too far from your own particular situation.

What I say here is based on my own experiences and some from talking with other praise leaders; some things the Lord taught me; and others I just learned the hard way. All of it, you might say, is my opinion, not necessarily a word from the Lord. If you read something here that rings your bell, seek the Lord and see if it is really for you. I know I can relate to ideas that are not necessarily for me.

FOR PASTORS

When starting a new church it is important that whoever leads the praise be anointed, and the Holy Spirit is upon them when they lead. There are many that have good intentions and even some real ability to play or sing, but are they anointed for that job? Sometimes the anointing is easy to see on someone.

Is their character ready to handle the warfare around a new church and praise in general? It is easy to jump-the-gun, in a manner of speaking, and put someone in a position for which they are not yet ready. Don't let someone's willingness or enthusiasm influence the decision on who is to lead. The anointing with the Holy Spirit must be the reason. The presence of the Holy Spirit is the activating of the anointing (see Luke 4:18).

If there doesn't seem to be anyone who fits that description, then don't have live music. Use CDs or tapes, but don't just throw someone into that fire. If they are not called and anointed to do it, the enemy will cut them into pieces. Not right away, to be sure, but in time. The enemy recognizes a leader without authority in a minute and will take full advantage of it. The best example of someone being in the wrong place is Saul and David. Saul was anointed king as a result of the people demanding a leader. They wanted to be like other nations with a man as king. After Saul disobeyed God, David was anointed by Samuel to lead Israel. I feel David was God's first choice all along, but the people wanted a king before God or David was ready. When it was time for David to take his rightful place on the throne, there had to be a war to end Saul's reign and put David in his place. There is much more to this story, but the point is, God has a man for every job if we can stand to wait for His choice.

If someone is leading praise because there was no one else to take the job, there is a good chance that person will be in the way of the one that God has chosen. I've only met one man in all these years who was able to lead praise in a church and continue to look for the one God would send. The church enjoyed his leading, but he knew there was someone else coming. When God's choice came, he gracefully stepped down and continued to praise God from the congregation. His name was Wes Warlen. I mention his name to honor such humility, and because he has gone on to praise the Lord from a much higher place than the stage.

Watching a praise leader in a home group will give you an idea of when they might be ready for the church. The sign to look for: everyone will follow a true leader without any cheerleading needed. If there must be a consistent goading of the people to enter in, or the people are just sitting with blank stares on their faces, this one is not ready yet. I know I don't need to say this, but everything written in this book always includes women.

Be sure you know the praise leader well in the Spirit as well as the natural. Being able to sing or play an instrument is not enough qualification. Be sure to keep that relationship ongoing, and if you see struggle in his or her family life, that is a sign they may not be carrying enough God-given authority for the job. The attack that comes on a musician that is prematurely leading frequently starts with problems in the family.

Be watchful for those that believe the church is their venue for success. The church becomes their stage and a control spirit may soon follow. I'm sad to say that there are a greater number of musicians and singers who want their own agenda than those that are broken and poured out before the Lord. If you can keep from over-stressing the need to have someone on stage leading praise, your patient determination to follow God will detour that control spirit. Sometimes agendas will start with a heart to help.

When David played before Saul, it drove demons away. If the musicians in the church play with ambition or agenda, it will attract demons to the stage and the church. (There is more on this in the chapter called "The Musician and the Church.")

For Praise Leaders

If you are the potential praise leader, be sure to get to know the pastor well. Knowing his heart will help you to lead the praise God wants from that particular church. The Holy Spirit will guide the praise direction of a church to fulfill the calling that is on that church. For example, I led praise in a church that had a heart for Israel. Much of the worship had an Israeli feel to it.

Another church had a warring heart because of the neighborhood it was in, so there was more attention paid to battling in the Spirit. Still a praise leader must remember that the preaching of the Word is what the people will take home and impart into their lives. Faith comes by hearing the Word; there is no mention of praise in Romans 10:17. Thankfulness and praise are what we all freely give to Jesus.

If you are leading in a church and the pastor won't let you move freely in the Spirit, there is a good chance he does not trust your discernment. Go before the Lord and ask Him to reveal whatever hidden things you cannot see. You may be unconsciously moving in your own agenda and the pastor doesn't want to hurt your feelings by telling you. He may be afraid of losing the only praise leader he has, or just not sure about how to approach you. Because you move freely at home or in a small group, does not make it right for the church. The pastor is not the only one God will talk to concerning your church, but he will be the final decision. Even if the pastor is wrong, God will not bypass him in favor of you. I speak this from hard learned experience.

In the coming move of the Lord to salvation there will be many musicians trying to answer a call they don't understand. A sound will call them to the Lord, or a song in the spirit that they cannot resist. If the musicians that are now in the church try to protect it through jealousy, they will stop and even kill the move of the Lord for the craftsmen, artists, and musicians needed to help in the harvest that is coming. The job of the Levite is to watch and protect, but not against the move of the Lord.

What if the People Just Won't Enter In?

There are many reasons for a group of people to be occasionally resistant to praise. The Lord gave me an open vision one day about the praising people of God. He showed me a line of homeless and hungry people waiting to get into a soup kitchen. The price is grateful praise and the food is the Word of God. He showed this to me as a picture of His church. If you've been starving, you will gladly pay and the food will taste real good. It is easy to feed hungry people.

On the other hand, if the people are not really hungry, they will be much more reluctant to be grateful for their meal in advance. When people are hungry for God, they gladly pay the price of praise. They also trust in what the Lord is going to give them after they have made their offering.

The only negative in this is that hungry people will enter into praise enthusiastically and jump at the chance to bless the

Lord. This will sometimes leave the praise leader with the false impression they are the greatest leader in the world. This is quite a trap, but it can be avoided by humbling yourself before the Lord regularly. Hungry people will cause praise leaders and musicians to long for that kind of reaction every time praise is led.

The local church can sometimes be complacent concerning praise when they have heard the same band and the same songs for months on end. It is important to keep fresh in your search for what the Spirit is doing today and not try to repeat something because it was anointed in the past. I'm not referring to the songs you sing, but the freshness of the anointing.

Another reason people don't enter into praise is that the music is real bad and they just can't say one more time, "bless their hearts, the band tries real hard." Even a hungry person will resist real bad food. At the risk of sounding repetitious, the praise leader must be anointed with the Holy Spirit on him or her. If those two things are present, the people will enter in. I have heard the statement made, "if our musicians were better there would be more of the presence of God." That should be changed to, "if our musicians were anointed for this task, there would be more presence." We all know that musicianship has nothing to do with the presence of God, but anointing with the Holy Spirit does. This allows the Holy Spirit to pick the musicians He wants to lead praise and not the church.

Still another reason is the band and the music is too slick for the people to feel like they can get real before God. Slick means professional, and professional means knowing your limitations and always staying beneath them to give the illusion of perfection. I know that I am constantly trying to perfect one thing or another. If it's not my guitar sound, it's the PA system or whatever. It's good to improve, but there must always be room for the Spirit to carry you to a place you have never been before. Trying to get to that place is usually wrought with uncharted roads. It will get unpredictable at times and even messy. If you are too afraid of looking unsure or immature as a musician, you may not be able to get into the deep places of the Spirit. This will most definitely cause the people to not enter into real praise.

If you start praise by looking for what the Spirit is doing, He will show you how to sing the same song with a fresh anointing. If you become uneasy with searching for the Spirit, it's not uncommon for the musicians to turn towards entertainment to keep things going (There is more on entertainment in the chapter called *"Entertainment"*).

PERFECTING PRAISE TIMES

I played in a church one time and the band and choir were well-known for the presence of the Lord coming when they sang. The church grew so much that they built a new building next to the old place they had. There was a constant effort in the band and choir to improve, and they grew in leaps and bounds as a result. There was more and more effort put in to how they performed the songs while complacency was setting in concerning the presence.

In the new building there was a large stage built to accommodate the ever growing and improving praise band. They also included a curtain that could be lowered before the praise started, so the people wouldn't see the large choir and band getting into their positions before the service. They had gone beyond improving the band and choir, and on to how all of it looked and how they wanted to be presented. They had become, "slick," or professional.

Just a side note here. When there is a concern about a spirit of performance getting into the church, it has more to do with the presentation of the performance than anything else. That can be found in as subtle a way as color coordinating the carpet with the seats. The spirit of performance is the endless striving to perfect something, until all the attention is focused on the performance over what is being said. In other words, when I focus on the way I sing a song more than what the song is saying, I'm performing something and not saying anything. The spirit of performance can easily hide in the appreciation of others who see how much hard work it takes to get that perfected.

Speakers can go through this, too. If there is a greater emphasis on how you speak rather than what you say, it will lose its impact.

There were complaints from some about the curtain and it being too much like a show. Others said it was nice not seeing the choir enter the stage for all the commotion it created. As you can imagine, opinions were flying.

After enough complaints, there was a leadership meeting called to discuss the use of the curtain before praise started. One night before a rehearsal, the curtain had been raised, and somehow the motor that raised it started to overheat By the time the band and choir had gone home and the church was empty, the motor reached a dangerous temperature and began to burn. This triggered the sprinkler system and saturated this new building with water, ruining the curtain and the seats and carpet.

The pastor, being a humble man, fell on his face in front of his entire congregation, as they sat on warped seats now bolted to a cement floor. He cried out to God to forgive them for focusing on their building more than Him. The rest of the church joined him and though the place didn't look so good for a while, the Spirit was all over them. The church looks great now; all redone; with two new additions. Humility and the presence of the Lord accomplished the tasks.

I know this is an overdone example of "slick", but I wanted to show how this idea has no end. Once you start on a trail of perfecting presentation you will ultimately abandon the purpose. This is what the Pharisees did. They perfected the doing of the Law over the heart of it.

IF I MINISTER TO THE LORD AT HOME, SHOULD I BE LEADING IN CHURCH?

Most believers will respond to praise if it is anointed. If what you are leading seems anointed to you but no one else feels that way, (excluding faithful friends that can't bear to tell you the truth) then that is the answer. Your praise is for you and the Lord alone. Go home and minister to the Lord, and don't worry about leading His people. The anointing breaks the yoke. That means without the anointing, there will be yokes on the people. Sometimes leaders that are in the wrong place at the wrong time can actually put yokes on a congregation. It is not horrible to imagine offering praise to the Lord by yourself. He is an awesome audience.

WHEN DOES CORPORATE PRAISE BECOME INTIMATE?

Deep love for Jesus is a personal thing, like the love between husband and wife. It's alright to show others that you love your spouse, but there are many expressions of love that are not for public meetings. Remember "worship" means to bow low and to serve God. Praise is what we are required to offer to the Lord and the expressions of it are pointed out in Scripture (see the chapter on "Seven Hebrew Words for Praise").

Sometimes our personal expressions of adoration to the Lord are almost uncomfortable to others when you are leading. If you lead a group of believers into your own personal style of intimacy, then you are leading by your own opinion and not the Spirit. That kind of leading will frequently bring condemnation on a people that already feel they don't measure up spiritually.

It is quite another matter when you're just one of many glorifying the Lord. They may express their intimacy to God in a number of ways, but to lead a group into a personal relationship is a little like trying to publicly tell someone how to be intimate with their spouse.

Another point to think about is that believers are the bride to be. We are not yet married to the Savior. Though spiritual intimacy in the Lord may be nothing like it is on earth with married couples, none of us really know what it will be like until *after* the wedding. I'm basing this on God's law that forbids premarital intimacy, and that the wedding supper of the Lamb has yet to come.

I have mentioned this to some true lovers of the Lord and found them getting pretty angry about the idea of not being completely intimate with the Lord until after marriage. I'm not making a doctrine by what I say, but an observation for praise leaders. I don't want to quench anyone's expression of love for

Jesus, only bring sensitivity to leaders who need to stay focused on the Spirit.

To be skillful in leading praise, you must discern what is happening all around you. You must learn how far you can go and when to do it when you lead God's people. That can only happen when the Spirit leads you. Your job is to facilitate by sounding the trumpet (metaphorically speaking) as a call to the Lord, like the musicians did at the foot of Mt. Sinai when Moses tried to bring Israel to meet their God. You are not responsible for what they do when they get there.

DOES BEING A GOOD MUSICIAN HAVE AN AFFECT ON PRAISE?

Yes, it does, but the effect it has may come as a surprise. My classical guitar teacher once said to me, "The reason you practice is so when music decides to use you, you can offer an ever increasing vocabulary." Though he didn't know the Lord, I feel he was prophesying to me about my future as a worshiper.

It is not what the Holy Spirit knows about music that limits me, it's what I refuse to experience through time with my instrument that limits me. We must offer our best to the Lord at all times. If you have played for one year, then you must offer the best you have for one year. If you have played for thirty years, then offer what you have gained from thirty years of practice and hard work. All musicians that carry the burden of music in their hearts should know we have all received something slightly different from the Creative One. Each one has something unique to offer the Lord. Think of the gift of music like the parable of the talents Jesus spoke about in Matthew 25:15-27. The most that can be done with this talent is to increase it. No matter if you start with five talents or just one. The least that can be done with a talent is to gain interest with it. That's not the worst thing that can be done, just the least.

Another reason it is important to play well as a praise leader is the anointing has a tendency to rise and fall during praise times. At the high times every musician sounds great. It's at the low times that the struggle starts. If your musicianship cannot carry you through the down times while you wait for the Spirit to move again, a tentative feeling begins to go out over the people and they sense the leader is groping. Before you know it, someone will try to save this ambiguous situation and a spirit of control will take over. If you have enough skill in your playing, it will have a calming affect on the people while you wait (skill meaning knowing music well). The next rise of the Spirit will soon be there.

Yet another very important reason to play well is playing the instrument is praise. Music was not intended to accompany singing, singing was intended to accompany music. Many times in Scripture we are instructed to praise the Lord. Almost every time the phrase "I will sing praise" or just "sing praise," is used in the Psalms, the Hebrew word for praise is "zamar". This word means: *"to pluck the strings of an instrument or strike with the hand"*. The definition goes on to say: *"this form of praise can be accompanied with singing"*. Playing the instrument is the praise; singing is for accompanying that playing. This may come as a bit of a surprise, but God did not invent musicians to be accompaniment for singers, though that is a mindset for much of our culture.

If you feel that your playing only has to be good enough to backup your singing, then a big part of praising God has been left out. David was known to have been able to chase demons away with his skillful harp playing. The word "skillful" means: *"to know, to perceive"*; it relates to knowing something or someone intimately. His intimacy with music facilitated his intimacy with God, which caused demons to flee when he entered that place with confidence. That kind of heartfelt knowing music can unseat demons. On the other hand, over-playing because you can, or just being insensitive to the moment, can do the opposite. A musician that plays way more than the song or situation calls for can actually attract demons. Overplaying or doodle-in, as I call it, will trigger competition, jealousy, and later selfish ambition. You can cast these demons out and when someone starts overplaying again, they come right back.

Much of the battle praise leaders face on Sunday morning is the musical war that is taking place on stage. With the varying degrees of musicianship that often make up a Sunday morning praise band, there is a silent war going on. Many bands have no idea of how much that war is quenching the move of the Spirit.

CAN I HELP A TALENTED PERSON WITH THE DECISION BETWEEN CHURCH AND THE WORLD?

Those that have a high level of talent are given this gift for a few reasons. One of the reasons is to see just what they will do with it. All gifts and talents are given to glorify God, but sometimes they are used by the Lord in the world.

Most everyone that has the goods to try at the "big time" will do just that, sooner or later. Trying to talk them out of it will be fruitless. Only God can stimulate a desire to sacrifice all to praise Him.

Not every talented musician or singer is meant for leading praise, and if they are, it doesn't mean it is for all time. Some people are meant to be in front of others in some form of entertaining them. Remember the Hebrew word "halal" means: *"to be bright, to shine, to be famous"*. Halal is one of the Hebrew words for praise (see "Seven Hebrew Words for Praise"). It can bring praise to God for someone to be famous. Being famous is not sinful, but the route that must be taken to get famous will often awaken a spirit of selfish ambition, jealousy, strife, and competition. Holding that position of fame will then become your quest. That is when it stops bringing glory to God.

My best advice for this is love this gifted person even if you feel they are making a mistake. The love they receive from the church will stay with them during the sifting (see Luke 22:31-32).

WHAT IF OUR CHURCH DOESN'T HAVE ANY TALENTED MUSICIANS?

There is almost always someone who is gifted in music in every gathering of believers. That doesn't mean they will come forward and say, "Hi, I'm a talented musician." One gifted musician will generally attract another and so on. If there is an overabundance of people willing to play or lead but having no real gifting, then the talented ones sitting in the crowd will keep silent. They are silent for two reasons. 1) They are not needed; there are too many on stage already. 2) They don't want to play with real bad musicians.

If you have ever played tennis before, you will know that it is a bad idea to play with a beginner if you have some experience. It is best to play with someone that is equal or better, so you grow and sharpen your own skills. The same is with music. A good musician regularly playing in a bad band runs the risk of losing the ability to play in a steady tempo, play in tune, and the desire to improve.

A good musician will not come forward if there are too many musicians lacking the desire to improve on stage. The problem is not average musicianship in the church, it is a lack of passion to grow and learn. We frequently mistake loving to be on stage with loving to play.

INTERCESSION

I could spend a lot of time talking about intercession and praise. The twenty-four elders surrounding the throne of God with bowls of incense (prayers of the saints) and harps, prove that praise and prayer exist in the same person (see Revelation 5:8).

It is very important that a praise band have intercessors to stand with them. My wife has stood with me on occasion and interceded right on stage with me. This happened as a result of the Spirit leading us all into something new. However, like all things that are new to us, there are start-up problems. To make a very long story short, if you don't already have intercessors on stage with you, I don't advise starting. Let me try to explain.

There is something that happens to most people when they get on a stage, even a very small and humble stage. An unexplainable thing happens when you get up in front of others. You become very self-conscious and may find yourself acting like a caricature of yourself. What others have said about you is what you will begin to relate to on stage. For example: if someone told you they thought you were very funny, you will start to act funny when you get on stage. If others have remarked about liking the way you praise God, you will find yourself trying to act like you are praising when you're on stage, thus making the stage a place of unreality and not truth at all. Remember the Greek mindset is, the stage is for acting.

Not everyone becomes an actor when on stage, but it does take some time in that position to get over feeling watched. The most difficult part of this type of intercession is when intercessors become conscious of themselves, they become a distraction and their intercession has the opposite effect.

On the positive side, intercession done right with the musicians can have an awesome effect on the praise time, whether it is on the stage or off. It will be something like turbo-charging the band. Praise can take off like never before. However, if the leader wants to turn a corner it is not always wisdom to have the turbo-charger going. You may crash and burn. Care must be taken so that the intercession doesn't try to drive the praise.

Just recently my wife has taken to gathering the intercessors in another room, far away from the stage; far enough away that she cannot even hear what is going on in the church. The intercession has become more accurate and deeper in the Spirit. When we talk about what happened in the Spirit later, we often find that the intercessors were praying the very words that were being sung spontaneously from stage that day.

I feel it is safe to say, don't make any hard and fast rules concerning where to do intercession. Just intercede when and where the Spirit of God instructs. We are seeing the need for a leader in the intercession to keep it focused. When passionate people for God come together, they will have many worthwhile subjects to pray about. But if the goal is to intercede for the church or the praise band, then those prayers need to stay focused.

How Can I Change a Traditional Praise Time?

The word "tradition" means: *"giving up, giving over, a giving over which is done byword of mouth or in writing, that is, tradition by instruction"*. We do things in a traditional way because we just always have. This Greek definition of tradition goes on to say that the precepts of the Law of Moses were orally transmitted down through the generations, and the expansions and additions they added to the Law were to be obeyed with equal reverence, as was the Law.

To bring change to the traditional way praise is always done, you must first have another (anointed) way well practiced. "Well practiced" means to practice following the Spirit in as many ways as He leads. The church is not the place to experiment. The school, the small group, or one person at home is where the Holy Spirit will show new ways to praise the Lord.

Some other suggestions to help bring change to the traditional praise times are: Don't rely on the visible reactions of the people to know if you're following the Holy Spirit. Your reward is not in their faces, and often the strongest response to the Spirit is silence.

Try making little changes in the way you sing a well-known song. It breaks a habit pattern and an expectancy that has been unconsciously set up. Tell the band to be ready for anything. You'll get some complaints at first, but if the Spirit falls they will love the change. The change is to interrupt the traditional mindset and open the door to the Spirit, not to upset the people.

Start the praise a different way once in awhile. When we . begin to expect the unexpected, then the Spirit has a platform already set for Him.

Example

a. Have someone else in the praise group start the worship time.

b. Try singing your prayers to start with.

c. Start with a victory shout and open gratitude to God.

d. Ask the Lord to give you divinely inspired ways to begin moving toward the throne.

e. Write praise songs from your own heart. Don't be afraid to sing of your failures as well as your victories. David did. (Don't be morbid, and always show a way to victory.)

There are many other ways to break traditional ideas in the praise time, but be sure you are not acting out of rebellion to the way things are, but as an act of obedience to the Holy Spirit.

If you feel your musical ability is so limited that you could not take such chances, don't forget you still have an imagination. Face your fears of inadequacy and begin to express yourself before God as David did. It's the heart that God is interested in.

Again, practice all this at home or in a small group before trying to get the body to go along with your experiments. They will better appreciate what you are doing if you have already been through a few trials and errors.

TRYING TO MAKE IT PERFECT

I know from my own "I gotta perfect this thing" message that musicians in general are always trying to get something or another better. It's either the sound of their instrument, or the way they sing, or the PA system and so on and so on. Many times it's just getting the arrangement of a song better. No matter what we are doing there is at least a measure of perfection being attempted in a praise band.

This try at perfection can also be the heart of many arguments, both vocal and silent, in the band. There is always someone who has more experience or knowledge than another and the feelings of inadequacy or intolerance can find their way into the music itself. The battle is no longer in the heavens, but on the stage. This can nullify your efforts to touch the Lord.

Perfection, in Greek and in Hebrew means to be complete, finished, or strengthened, like when fruit comes into its perfection, it is ripe, or complete. I've been playing the guitar for forty years and though I've learned much, I have even more yet ahead.

So the idea of real perfection on an instrument of music is impossible in this lifetime. What this means is there are some musicians that are more mature than others. They are the ones that need to help the others through rough spots in the music and encourage them when they get it.

If you are the musical director and someone else is more musically experienced than you, humble yourself and ask for help. If you are the music leader and the most experienced, then help the others with patience always looking for improvement.

Even the slightest improvement should be noticed and noted (I don't mean overstated compliments). If there is no measurable improvement in someone you have had input with, then there may be another problem under the surface. In any case it's time to ask that person why they are not showing any signs of growth. If this person is a good musician and just bored with playing with lesser players, then the question "why are you here?" should be addressed. The answer should be "to praise the Lord."

If any musician is on stage because they feel some kind of obligation to the church or the other musicians, they will eventually resent that place and become a subtle drain on the life of the other players. It has the potential to drain the spirit life out of the rest of the musicians and even members of church that identify with praise more than preaching.

There are many more scenarios I could address on this subject of attempted perfection in the praise band, but none are more important than this. If any attempt to perfect the music, the musicians, or the equipment gets in front of the search for the Holy Spirit's guidance, then there will be a spiritual deficit in the praise time. Jesus is the perfecter of our faith (see Hebrews 12:2). It takes faith to grow in Spirit and in music. He will bring us into the maturity level needed to reach the heavens with praise.

> O Lord, come quickly to Your temple (see Malachi 3:1-4).

THE TAMBOURINE

I have been in many services where the tambourine was used in the band or by dancers with an understanding of how to play it and use it as an act of celebration. I have also been in services where the tambourine was the most distracting instrument played. Some churches make rules about not playing this instrument and others give tambourines out at the door. I personally have some reservations about the instrument being played during praise time because of the volume and power that little round drum with brass rings has. It is louder than any instrument on stage, including the sound system. Every musician that hears a tambourine in the crowd is automatically distracted from the cadence set by the band. This very small instrument is capable of disrupting and even stopping the band from being able to play together.

The technical reason is the short distance that the tambourine is away from the stage causes a time delay. Even if the tambourine player is great, he or she will inevitably be behind the tempo of the band. To the tambourine player, it sounds like you're right on with the band, but you are not. By the time two, three, or more begin to play, there is a mass of rhythm patterns coming at the stage and some bands cannot ignore this force. It will pull the band off and sometimes they will begin to fight internally about why they can't play together, not realizing it could be an outside influence distracting them.

With all that in mind, there is a spiritual reason, too. The tambourine or timbrel was frequently used in Canaanite fertility cults. It was considered inappropriate for the Temple. It is not mentioned with the instruments that David instructed the Levites to use in the Tabernacle. That may be because of its use in cult rituals.

When Miriam took the timbrel and went out rejoicing (see Exodus 15:20), she was setting a cadence that others could follow. Other women then followed her, playing timbrels and dancing and singing. She was the first to play the tambourine for a godly reason, but the purpose was to play a loud enough instrument that many could hear it and come into cadence with it. She was setting a cadence for others to follow.

If you are playing a tambourine during a praise time in a church, then you are attempting to set a cadence for others to follow. That cadence will be different from the cadence the band is trying to set. If many are playing tambourines at the same time, then there are many requests being made to follow their own cadence. You may have heard the phrase, "He plays to his own drummer." That is just a clever way of saying he refuses to come into cadence or rhythm with others. He is considered rebellious. It's interesting to note, Miriam's name means rebellion.

There are Scriptures like I Samuel 10:5 where the tabret is mentioned. However, this was one of the instruments used by a band of prophets coming down from the mountains. This was a timekeeper meant for that band.

I was leading a praise session in a small church one time, and a sweet lady had a tambourine and was playing with all her might. Every once in a while she would get right with the band and there was almost a good feel about it. Then suddenly she would start looking around to see what was happening and get way off from the band. Just then, I started getting a prophetic song for that congregation and when I tried to get the band to quiet down a little to do this song, the tambourine lady kept right on playing full volume. The people never noticed that I was trying to quiet down, so they kept right on partying to the beat of the tambourine. I never got a chance to give this word to the church and eventually gave up trying. At that point, that sweet lady controlled the whole church and nothing short of yelling at her could have stopped it. I gave the word to the pastor later and he almost wept because the church truly needed to hear this word.

My personal feelings about the tambourine are, in the hands of a percussionist that instrument can be a very effective tool for celebration, praise, and warring in the Spirit. I've never seen a percussionist play the tambourine constantly, but only as an accent instrument in certain sections of a song. Then he always concentrates on the drummer to play right with him. He never creates a cadence of his own. For use in organized dances and for special events, this is a great instrument. For use in a band by a percussionist, I'm all for it. For anyone who feels like playing the tambourine during praise time, I'm not all for it. This is just one man's opinion.

THE CROSS

The last thing I want to mention is the cross. I'm not going to give you another sermon on this awesome subject, but only something to ponder. If you are a praise leader, musician, or a hopeful, you have been used in some way to fulfill the vision of another. You've also been offended, and if not, you soon will be.

It is almost impossible to live with music in any form without drawing comments that wound and those who use. The Lord has shown me something that has taken twenty-one years to completely realize.

After too many years of trying to please men, I realized my life had been given away or in some cases actually stolen. I asked myself: "Have I truly walked in the call of God for my life, or have I only been trying to fulfill the visions and expectations of others?" I hated the answer to that, so I started trying to get my life back. During that process I became very angry with all those who only wanted what I could do and didn't really have an enduring love for me. I knew that all of this was the result of a man-pleasing spirit and a religious spirit in me trying to destroy what God intended.

Just then the Lord began to reveal something about the cross I never saw before, and it brought great comfort and assurance to me.

The call on the life of Jesus was made clear when He said,

"The Spirit of the Lord is upon me, because he hath anointed me to preach the gospel to the poor; he hath sent me to heal the brokenhearted, to preach deliverance to the captives, and recovering of sight to the blind, to set at liberty them that are bruised,

**To preach the acceptable year of the Lord"
(Luke 4:18-19 KJV).**

I knew I was one of those He came to set free, as well as giving me spiritual eyes to see. Still there was an even deeper message He wanted me to recognize. Then He showed me this.

Jesus doesn't mention dying on the cross as a part of the call on His life in this Luke 4 Scripture. He only spoke of the cross to His disciples after three years. That's because He didn't come to hang on a cross, but to preach the good news and set men free and proclaim the acceptable year of the Lord. His life and ministry were stolen from Him by the spirit of religion (the Pharisees) and the spirit of this world (man-pleasing, living for man instead of God).

Judas wanted his expectation of a humanistic Christ fulfilled. The zealots wanted Messiah to fulfill their vision of power to kill the Roman oppressors. The Pharisees wanted praise for their outward shows of piousness, and His disciples just didn't want to loose Him. All the visions and expectations that others wanted Jesus to fulfill were hung on a cross and died with Him. He could only be what God intended Him to be—the Savior of the world, not the fulfillment of the agendas of man.

I'm not comparing myself in any way to the Savior. He remained perfect and true to the call on His life where I have failed many times. He only fulfilled the will of His Father and I have tried to fulfill the will of men. However, the cure is the same-the cross. What I had to learn was to embrace my cross. I also had to repent and say: I forgive... Then the Lord reminded me that more was done after the resurrection than was done before the cross (see John 21:25). The reason the Lord tells me to take up my cross is so I can spiritually die and have a resurrection. It is only after all those offenses have been completely realized and forgiven and hung on a cross that the real power we have longed for comes.

But if the Spirit of Him who raised Jesus from the dead dwells in you, He who raised Christ Jesus from the dead will also give life to your mortal bodies through His Spirit who indwells you (Romans 8:11).

Conclusion

Since God uses the foolish things to confound the wise (see 1 Corinthians 1:20), it is safe to say striving for perfection and working to make yourself look good to others may only serve to disqualify you. If you are a praise leader or hoping to be one, then you have agreed to stand between God and His people. This is when you automatically give up your right to refuse God's process of making you transparent. He is not looking for a door to heaven, but a window without glass.

May God richly bless you and pay heed to your cry of praise all the days of your life.

appendix
seven hebrew words of praise

LEARNING TO DANCE BEFORE THE LORD

When I was first studying these Hebrew words, I would tell others how they should set aside their inhibitions, and just give it up before the Lord. "Just let go and dance like a wild man!" was often coming from me.

One day shortly after that I was going to play a concert at a Spirit-filled church. Feeling confidant, I believed that at some point during this concert I would break into my newly found knowledge of these praise words. As I started the concert I noticed that their reaction to the music was reserved. I made up my mind that they needed to hear my sermon on the seven Hebrew words of praise right away, and there was no time to delay.

When I got to the word "halal" I felt I heard the Lord say, "Do you want to be an imitator of Me?" As I was playing the guitar and teaching in-between licks, I managed to answer in my mind, "Yes, of course I want to imitate You." Quickly I heard, "Then get up and dance wildly before Me." I began to argue immediately, that I was playing the guitar and the wires hooked up to it were not long enough, and besides there would be no music for me to dance to.

Then came that silent period when you know that God is not going to argue or ask ten times. I looked out at a very reserved church and said, "I think the best way to show you what I mean by being joyful before the Lord, is to dance before God myself." I put my guitar down and slowly got up to a completely silent room and began to dance in circles. I felt like I danced for two hours, but I'm sure it was only seconds. On one or two of my spins I noticed that no one was reacting at all, and this whole idea was designed to make a fool out of me. After an eternity of dancing I thought I heard someone clapping his or her hands. Sure enough it was the pastor. Then others joined him, and before I could recover from dizziness, the whole church seemed to be caught up in the joy of the moment.

The pastor came to the front at that point and began to weep. He told his congregation that he had taught them the Word of God and that they knew well how to quote Scripture, but he had not taught them about the joy of the Lord. I sat back down in my chair exhausted from the ordeal and knew clearly what halal meant.

Many times in this book I referred to the Hebrew words that are used when the word "praise" is found in the Old Testament. I thought it might be useful to spell these out as I use them regularly. I learned them from Ray Hughes. He held a class on praise every Tuesday night in Nashville where we lived. I had already led praise for a few years at that point and couldn't imagine ever being able to learn anything more than I had already discovered accidentally. After several months of this class, I stole this information and I now present it to you as if I researched it myself. I did, however, look up all the words and all the Scripture references to see if they were true. They are true.

The Bible is full of the words praise, bless, or glory. Whenever these words are used they can mean one of many Hebrew words. The following is a list of only seven words. This is not an exhaustive list by any means. All these definitions were taken from the *Hebrew Greek Key Study Bible KJV* and *Strong's Concordance* of the Bible. (There are many Greek words for praise as well, but I'm only using the Hebrew.)

The first word for "praise" in the Hebrew is one of the most important words I found. That is because the heart of the word is to confess your sins. The root of the word is to have an intimate knowing of God. (These words are not in any particular order; just in the order Ray taught them.)

1. YADAH=

Praise, thank, thanksgiving, cast (throw), Genesis 29:35, when Leah had her fourth son, she raised her hands in praise to the Lord, and called him Judah (praise). This is the first time anyone was recorded raising their hands in praise for their blessings: Praise as a result of blessing. Psalm 60:30-31, David is saying his confession of praise and thanksgiving is more pleasing to God than his sacrifice. This praise also includes public confession of sin: Psalm 32-5 To confess, to sing praise, to sing, etc. essentially it is to acknowledge the word of God and man's character.

YADA=

The root of YADAH which means to be intimately acquainted with someone, or God. To understand or acquire knowledge; to know; to discern; (learning to discern God's heart). To know by learning and experiencing. Knowing through the senses, by investigating and proving. To become acquainted in a sexual way to make oneself known; to be familiar; to reveal oneself. This Hebrew word occurs 995 times in the O.T. Knowledge gained through the senses.

2. TOWDAH=

Praise, thank offering, means to praise no matter what your circumstances. Lifting your hands in praise begins the breaking in the one praising that is needed to defeat the oppression of the enemy. Raising the hands is a sign of surrender, signaling the enemy that you are given over to God. Psalm 100, Psalm 50:23, Jeremiah 17:26, Psalm 56:12.

3. HALAL=

Praise, boast, celebrate, clamorously foolish, to shine, hence to make show, to rave, sing, rage, renowned, all these forms of praise are offered in an attitude of delight. To be bright, to be splendid, to be praised, to be famous, to cause to shine, to make bright, to give light, to deserve praise, radiance is at the heart...It is the root word of Hallelujah. HALAL is used 113 times in the Old Testament Psalm 149:1, Jeremiah 31:7, Psalm 69:30, Psalm 22:22-25, Psalm 48:8. Jesus came to bring HALAL praise to the Father. This is a word for describing God. (There are instances where the word is applied to human beings. Genesis 12:15, II Samuel 14:25, I Kings 20:11, Psalm 63:11, Proverbs 31:28, 31.)

When David brought the Ark of the Covenant back to Israel, 'he danced wildly in front of it. He was praising in HALAL praise. In that time, it was traditional for the conquering army returning home to take a prisoner and strip him and make him dance in front of the king that conquered him. That is what David was doing when he (king of Israel) stripped himself and danced like a fool in front of the King that had conquered him.

This was also the praise that the heavenly host did when coming down out of Heaven to celebrate the birth of Jesus. (This is the praise that draws the most objections.)

4. BARAK=

Praise, kneel, bless, to do with motion. To confess, to thank, to use the hands, or to bow the knee, to revere, worship, salute, to bless God in an act of adoration.

Judges 5:2-3, Psalm 103:1: **"BLESS THE LORD O MY SOUL"** means to bow before the Lord O my soul. Psalm 72:15: The motion given in BARAK is bending the knee and blessing the King that supplies all your needs. There is usually no vocal expression in BARAK praise, but has to do with physical movement. This word is used 330 times in the OT Genesis 1:22 God blessed them and said, be fruitful and multiply. God taught us how to bless by first blessing us.

5. SHABACH=

Praise, triumph, glory, commend, a loud adoration, proclaiming with a loud voice unashamed glory. Ecclesiastes 4:2, Psalm 145:4, Psalm 147:12. Out of this shout comes triumph, actually shouting love unto God. To calm anger (see Proverbs 29:11), To still the waves, to soothe with praises (see Psalm 62:3). Jesus calmed the waves while in the boat with His disciples with this.

Though it may seem unlikely that a shout could have a calming affect on the turmoil of this life, it does just that. Letting go with a shout of praise will often bring a peace and a stilling of the torment the enemy puts on the people of God.

Psalm 63:1-3: In this Psalm, David is referring to SHABACH when he is saying **"Thus will I bless Thee"** for the loving kindness of God. There are many expressions of love unto God, and this is just one of them. When we shout the victory of love for God, we break the hold of the enemy. We are not only loving God, but also proclaiming it to all that would hear.

Psalm 117:1, Isaiah 12:6: Voice of triumph. Psalm 89:15: **"How blessed are the people that know the joyful sound."**

JOYFUL SOUND=earsplitting shout of joy. Trumpet blast...

6. ZAMAR=

Praise, sing praise with the instrument, means to touch with fingers the strings of an instrument, or to pluck a stringed instrument in celebration. Used in poetry, singing can be involved. Music was given to render praise unto God. Psalm 33:2, Psalm 71:2, II Samuel 22:50, Psalm 61:8, Psalm 66. Though the word "sing" is used, it means zamar.

ZAMAR was the praise that David offered when playing for Saul to rid him of the tormenting spirit.

7. TeHILLAH=

Praise, laudation, or hymn of praise: It is the most used word for praise in the Old Testament.

Comes from the word HALAL that comes from the root word HALLELUJAH.

HALAL= strong expression.

TeHILLAH is the song the Lord sings to us, through us. The Christians sang TeHILLAH praise when they were being fed to the lions, and the Romans discontinued the practice when so many of the people in the stands were touched by God.

It is God's song being sung.

Psalm 40:3: A new song "MANY WILL SEE AND FEAR AND TRUST IN THE LORD,"

Psalm 22:3: God is enthroned on TeHILLAH praise.

Psalm 22:5, Psalm 33:1, Psalm 48:10, Psalm 62:2, Psalm 147:1, Deuteronomy 10:21: In all these Scriptures the word praise is TeHILLAH.

Isaiah 60:18 Gates means praise (TeHILLAH). The gate into His presence is TeHILLAH praise.

Isaiah 61:3: A garment of praise replaces a spirit of heaviness.

Paul sang this form of praise while chained in prison. God inhabited that praise and the chains fell, the prison doors were opened, and salvation came and set the captive free.

BONUS WORD

TePhillah=

This word means intercession for someone (see II Kings 19:4; Isaiah 37:4; Jeremiah 7:16, 11:14), prayer, entreaty, supplication, hymn. This is the most general Hebrew word for prayer in the Old Testament. Isaiah 56:7 states that God's house will be a , house of prayer. This was the Scripture Jesus was quoting when He drove out the moneychangers from the temple courtyard (see Matthew 21:13). This term meant a prayer that was set to music and sung in formal worship.

Another Hebrew word for intercession is "paga." It's a more intense intercession with the root meaning to bear down in prayer.

I put this word in these definitions as an extra word because intercession and praise are so closely related. I also believe that praise and the prophetic are closely related as well as tools for teaching and evangelism.

Music from
Don Potter

Remember
Remember is a new kind of project for Don Potter as it includes his wife, Christine, in what they describe as "the marrying of Scripture and music." Performed in an "inspired song" style, this collection of music and spoken Scripture is truly unique.

I Live Here
In 2004, Don gathered some of his production and musician friends in the Nashville recording community to record *I Live Here*. This great team did a tremendous job bringing a fresh perspective to Don's new material as well as some songs from his MorningStar days.

While I Wait
Don recorded this collection of intimate instrumental worship in 2003 after moving back to Nashville.

Since the Fall
This is primarily a collection of songs Don recorded in Moravian Falls in 2003. Also included are several corporate worship songs captured live during the Levite Camp in Switzerland. All these songs are full of encouragement and exhortation.

All cds $14.00 each
visit www.donpottermusic.com
for more products and information